EQUAL JUSTICE UNDER LAW

New York Times Co. v. Sullivan:
FREEDOM OF THE PRESS OR LIBEL?

UNDER·LAW

SUPREME COURT MILESTONES

New York Times Co. v. Sullivan:

FREEDOM OF THE PRESS OR LIBEL?

SUSAN DUDLEY GOLD

Marshall Cavendish
Benchmark
New York

To Kiki O'Connell, master wordsmith and world-class friend

With special thanks to Professor David M. O'Brien of the Woodrow Wilson
Department of Politics at the University of Virginia for reviewing the text of this book.

Marshall Cavendish Benchmark
99 White Plains Road
Tarrytown, NY 10591
www.marshallcavendish.us

Library of Congress Cataloging-in-Publication Data
Gold, Susan Dudley.
New York Times Co. v. Sullivan : freedom of the press or libel? / by Susan Dudley
Gold.
p. cm. — (Supreme Court milestones)
Includes bibliographic references and index.
ISBN-13: 978-0-7614-2145-0
ISBN-10: 0-7164-2145-9
1. Sullivan, L. B.—Trials, litigation, etc. 2. New York Times Company—Trials, litiga-
tion, etc. 3. Trials (Libel)—United States. 4. Freedom of the press—United States. 5.
Libel and slander—United States. I. Title: New York Times Company versus Sullivan.
II. Title. III. Series.
KF228.N4G58 2006
342.7308'53—dc22
2005033983

Photo Research by Candlepants Incorporated

Cover: *Corbis*: Royalty-free

The photographs in this book are used by permission and through the courtesy of: *Dr.
Gwen Patton/Charles Conley Collection/Trenholm State Technical College Archives*: 1, 2, 3,
6; *Corbis*: Bettmann, 12, 27, 29, 30, 32, 42, 46, 55, 76, 80, 83, 85, 99, 111; Flip
Schulke, 15; 92. *Tommy Giles, Tommy Giles Photographic Service*: 20; *AP/Wide World
Photos*: 23, 34, 36; *The National Archives, London UK*: 44; *Columbia University Law
Library*: 64.

Series design by Sonia Chaghatzbanian
Printed in China
1 3 5 6 4 2

contents

AN AD IN THE *New York Times* SEEKING FUNDS FOR DR. MARTIN LUTHER
KING JR.'S DEFENSE BEGAN A SERIES OF COURT ACTIONS THAT LED TO THE
U.S. SUPREME COURT'S LANDMARK DECISION ON FREEDOM OF THE PRESS.

Introduction

NEW YORK TIMES V. SULLIVAN has been called the greatest First Amendment decision in American history. The case began with a full-page advertisement in the *New York Times* exhorting readers to "Heed Their Rising Voices." The headline came from a *New York Times* editorial published earlier that had urged Congress to "heed [the] rising voices" of peaceful demonstrators in the South demanding civil rights for black Americans.

Published on Tuesday, March 29, 1960, the ad recounted official mistreatment of students participating in two protests—one in Orangeburg, South Carolina, and a second in Montgomery, Alabama. It also detailed the arrests of civil rights leader the Reverend Dr. Martin Luther King Jr. and issued an appeal for funds to support the protesters' efforts. Sponsored by the Committee to Defend Martin Luther King and the Struggle for Freedom in the South, the ad featured a lengthy list of supporters, including well-known singers Nat King Cole and Mahalia Jackson, actors Harry Belafonte and Shelley Winters, baseball star Jackie Robinson, and former first lady Eleanor Roosevelt, among other celebrities. In addition, the names of twenty southern ministers were listed as endorsing the ad.

It was an impressive, and effective, pitch for funds. For many readers, the ad served as a wake-up call to aid in the civil rights struggle. They responded by sending thousands of dollars to the committee's New York address.

But the ad outraged white southern officials in Montgomery. They bristled at a northern newspaper's criticism of their handling of the civil rights unrest in the South. Montgomery commissioner L. B. Sullivan, who supervised the police department as part of his duties, saw the ad as a vicious and unjustified attack on him, his city, and the Montgomery police. He identified several errors in the ad's accounts of police brutality. In fact, the ad did contain errors, including the false claims that students were barred from the dining hall and that armed police ringed the college campus. Although the ad did not name Sullivan or any police official, Sullivan claimed its attacks against the Montgomery police department sullied his reputation as well as those of other officials. He sued the *New York Times* for libel and asked for a judgment of half a million dollars. Others lined up to file similar suits against the *Times*.

IMPASSIONED BATTLE OVER FREE SPEECH

What had begun as a fund-raising campaign for civil rights efforts soon mushroomed into an impassioned battle over freedom of speech and of the press. Did the Bill of Rights guarantee freedom of the press even when the material published was false? Could a public official quash erroneous statements he found objectionable? Did courts have the power to stop the press from printing material critical of authority but also inaccurate? The lawsuits that arose from the ad's publication eventually ended up in the highest court in the land. The U.S. Supreme Court's landmark decision on the matter in 1964 answered such questions and for the first time established guidelines on cases in which public officials sue for libel.

WHY a Lanpmark?

When the U.S. Supreme Court issued its ruling in *New York Times* v. *Sullivan* in 1964, the decision was hailed as a landmark. What made the case so significant? *Sullivan*, like many landmark decisions, achieved importance because the Court used the case to rule for the first time on a particular issue—in this case, libel. The *Sullivan* case gained stature, too, because of its impact on two principles central to America's democracy: freedom of the press and civil rights. As a result of *Sullivan*:

1. State libel laws must abide by the Constitution.
2. Public officials cannot collect damages for libel unless they can prove the statements were false, malicious, and intentionally hurtful ("actual malice").
3. A public official suing for libel must provide "clear and convincing proof" that the press or the speaker intentionally spread false, hurtful statements aimed at the official.
4. The Sedition Act of 1798 was ruled unconstitutional.
5. The First Amendment protects false statements as well as the truth.
6. Appeals courts may review evidence from trials to ensure that verdicts do not abridge free speech or freedom of the press.
7. Libel laws cannot be used to silence critics of governmental actions.

The case reinforced constitutional protections of free speech and freedom of the press. The Court's opinion, written by Justice William J. Brennan Jr., made it clear that the Constitution protects the right of citizens and the press to criticize public officials, even when what is said— or published—contains some falsehoods. According to the ruling, the court can award damages in such cases only when a public official can prove the speakers—or publications—acted with malice in making statements they knew were false or that they published with "reckless disregard" of whether the statements were true or false.

If people feared they would be punished merely for being wrong, they might well shrink from expressing any views at all, Justice Brennan wrote. Freedom of speech would become meaningless under those circumstances.

In his decision, Brennan said that "debate on public issues should be uninhibited, robust, and wide-open." Such debates, he added, "may well include vehement, caustic, and sometimes unpleasantly sharp attacks on government and public officials."

Some observers believe that had the Court not ruled against Sullivan, the civil rights campaign would have been set back considerably. In ruling the way it did, the Supreme Court thwarted southern officials' attempts to use civil libel laws to silence critics.

"If the national press could not safely report the activities of officials who were engaged in practices which denied blacks their basic civil rights, these wrongs might not have been corrected," legal expert Ellen K. Solender wrote about the case. Without detailed reports in the nation's newspapers and television's brutal images of violence against protesters, far fewer Americans might have supported the civil rights battle.

"The movement needed the *New York Times*," wrote Rodney A. Smolla in his book on libel and the media. "It needed the infant news broadcasts of CBS, NBC, and ABC, it needed the constant, virile, unsuppressed attention of a national press, in order to appeal to a national conscience."

Today, *Sullivan* stands as a safeguard of free speech and freedom of the press. The free exchange of ideas and the right of citizens and members of the press to criticize public officials openly—even if their statements are not always accurate—lie at the heart of American democracy.

ARKANSAS GOVERNOR ORVAL E. FAUBUS DISPLAYS A PHOTOGRAPH OF FEDERAL TROOPS, BAYONETS DRAWN, ESCORTING WHITE STUDENTS FROM CENTRAL HIGH SCHOOL IN 1957 DURING ATTEMPTS TO DESEGREGATE THE STATE'S PUBLIC SCHOOLS. FAUBUS OPPOSED PRESIDENT DWIGHT D. EISENHOWER'S DECISION TO CALL IN THE TROOPS.

one
A CALL TO ARMS

THE STRUGGLE FOR CIVIL RIGHTS became front-page news with the U.S. Supreme Court's 1954 decision that segregation in public schools violated the rights of black children. Five years after the ruling was issued, many southern communities continued to resist the order to desegregate schools. Protesters in Little Rock, Arkansas, backed by Governor Orval Faubus, blocked black students from entering the high school in the first attempts to desegregate schools in that city. Eventually, President Dwight D. Eisenhower called in federal marshals to protect the black students.

The push to desegregate the schools soon spread to other areas. Black citizens began demanding equal access to public buildings. Black students, many of whom attended black universities in the South, participated in sit-ins at drugstore lunch counters reserved for whites only. Other protesters, sometimes joined by white sympathizers, demonstrated at public swimming pools, on southern beaches, and in other areas closed to blacks.

Led by the young charismatic preacher, Dr. Martin Luther King Jr., the protesters sought racial equality. They gathered in peaceful demonstrations and marched through the streets to make their struggle known. Reaction against the protesters often escalated into violence. Members of the Ku Klux Klan and other racist groups, including some southern politicians and police officers, resisted the civil rights movement. Angry white mobs attacked black protesters and lynched black men. Terrorists among them bombed churches and schools, killing young children and spreading fear throughout black communities.

TV Broadcasts Struggle to Nation

In the 1950s and 1960s television for the first time connected Americans everywhere to what once might have been a regional story. The story was not restricted to the nightly news. Newspapers around the globe sent reporters to Montgomery, Alabama; Atlanta, Georgia; and other southern cities to give first-hand accounts of the growing movement and the often violent reactions of its opponents.

King became the target of white officials intent on preserving Southern segregation and their way of life. Along with other protesters, King was arrested, put in jail, and charged with traffic violations and other offenses. In December 1959, King announced plans to move from Montgomery, Alabama, to Atlanta, Georgia, to expand the fight for racial equality and integration. Once he had settled there, however, authorities in Alabama sought his extradition on perjury charges in connection with a state tax indictment. The civil rights leader agreed to return to Alabama to face trial.

Supporters rallied to King's aid. Three New York clergy announced a fund drive to raise $10,000 for King's defense. A short article about the drive appeared in the February 26, 1960, edition of the *New York Times*. Two of the three clergymen mentioned in the news article—the Reverend Dr. Harry Emerson Fosdick, minister emeritus of the Riverside Church, and the Reverend Dr. Gardner C. Taylor, president of New York City's Protestant Council—

TEENAGE GIRLS EXPRESS THEIR OPPOSITION TO DESEGREGATION BY SCREAMING OBSCENITIES OUTSIDE THEIR MONTGOMERY, ALABAMA, HIGH SCHOOL IN 1963.

held leadership posts in a group called the Committee to Defend Martin Luther King and the Struggle for Freedom in the South. The group sought donations to help King, fund the right-to-vote effort among black citizens, and support the student protesters. They placed a full-page ad in the *New York Times* on March 29 asking for donations.

"HEED THEIR RISING VOICES"

The ad's title, "Heed Their Rising Voices," ran across the page in big, bold type. In the upper right corner, a quotation from a *New York Times* editorial published on March 19, 1960, revealed where the headline originated: "The growing movement of peaceful mass demonstrations by

Negroes is something new in the South, something understandable. . . . Let Congress heed their rising voices, for they will be heard." The editorial had urged passage of the 1960 Civil Rights Act (a weakened form of the bill passed on April 21). The act created a Civil Rights Commission and levied fines against anyone interfering with a citizen's voting rights.

The ad told of several civil rights protests in the South and described mistreatment of student demonstrators. According to the ad, four hundred students in Orangeburg, South Carolina, were "forcibly ejected" from lunch counters in that city's business district when they tried to buy doughnuts and coffee. The students were "teargassed, soaked to the skin in freezing weather with fire hoses, arrested en masse and herded into an open barbed-wire stockade to stand for hours in the bitter cold," according to the ad.

The ad also described how students in Montgomery, Alabama, protested by singing "My Country, 'Tis of Thee" on the steps of the state capitol building. That action, according to the ad, led to the expulsion of student leaders and "truckloads of police armed with shotguns and teargas" who "ringed the Alabama State College Campus." The ad went on to relate that when the entire student body protested the actions, officials retaliated by padlocking their dining hall "in an attempt to starve them into submission."

Several other southern cities received mention in the ad—among them Tallahassee, Atlanta, Nashville, Savannah, and Memphis. In those cities and others, the ad said, American teenagers bravely stood against "the entire weight of official state apparatus and police power."

Continuing its strong indictment of the treatment of blacks in the South, the ad charged that "Southern violators of the Constitution" were "determined to destroy the one man who . . . symbolizes the new spirit now sweeping the South—the Rev. Dr. Martin Luther King, Jr." These "Southern violators," the ad continued, had resorted to intimidation and violence to stop King. They had bombed his home and assaulted him. They had also "arrested him seven times" on petty charges from speeding to loitering. King now stood charged with far more serious crimes— perjury and lying to the government on his income tax return. If convicted, he faced a ten-year jail sentence—a strategy designed to remove King from his leadership role in the civil rights battle, according to the ad. Such actions against King also discouraged others from stepping forward to lead the movement, the ad noted.

Defending Dr. King against the charge, the ad told readers, was critical and "an integral part of the total struggle for freedom in the South." Calling on "[d]ecent-minded Americans" to contribute to the cause, the ad urged supporters to send their dollars to the committee. "[T]his is one of those moments in the stormy history of Freedom," the ad concluded, "when men and women of good will must do more than applaud the rising-to-glory of others. The America whose good name hangs in the balance before a watchful world, the America whose heritage of Liberty these Southern Upholders of the Constitution are defending, is our America as well as theirs. . . .

"We must heed their rising voices—yes—but we must add our own."

Under these words, a smaller headline read, "Your Help Is Urgently Needed . . . NOW!!" Beneath that appeared four columns of names of prominent Americans, with a large number of celebrities among those listed. Singers Nat King Cole and Diahann Carroll; actors Marlon Brando, Sidney Poitier, and Harry Belafonte; baseball hero Jackie Robinson; and former first lady Eleanor Roosevelt all made the list in support of the campaign.

The names of twenty southerners, most of them black ministers, appeared in a separate listing further down the page under the heading, "We in the south who are struggling daily for dignity and freedom warmly endorse this appeal."

The ad ended with the committee's name, address, and list of officers and chairmen. A coupon for contributors to fill out and send with donations was printed in the lower right corner of the ad.

A POWERFUL AD

It was a powerful ad. Its creators intended to arouse intense emotions among readers. They chose words designed to move people to act, to reach into their pockets and give as much as they could to support Dr. King. Like many ads, this one exaggerated some of the claims. The ad also contained a few factual errors. The ad's claim that police had circled the college campus, for example, was not strictly true. In fact, the officers had guarded only three sides of the campus. Students had been expelled after participating in a sit-down strike at the courthouse lunch counter, not on the steps of the state capitol, as the ad had claimed. Alabama State College had never been "padlocked in an attempt to starve" students, according to college officials. Other errors in the ad—later acknowledged by both sides of the controversy—involved the song sung by students ("The Star-Spangled Banner," not "My Country, 'Tis of Thee").

After reviewing the ad, the *Times* advertising staff accepted it for publication. The committee paid the newspaper about $4,800 for the full-page advertisement. It went out in the national edition of the newspaper to about 650,000 readers. The *Times* delivered approximately 394 copies of the paper to Alabama, with about thirty-five newspapers distributed in Montgomery County.

The ad's strong words elicited a quick response among readers. Shortly after placing the ad in the *New York Times*, the committee began receiving contributions that far exceeded the cost of the ad.

The ad also caught the attention of Ray Jenkins, the city editor of the *Alabama Journal*. Across the street from the newspaper office, in Montgomery, Alabama, Martin Luther King Jr. sat in the courthouse, on trial for perjury. Noting King's name in the ad, Jenkins thought it might make a good story for his paper. He wrote a short article on the ad that appeared in the *Journal* on April 5, 1960. In his story, Jenkins reported that the ad contained several errors, which he considered to be minor. He listed the errors—the wrong song title, the expulsion of students for the wrong protest, and the "ringing" of the campus by police. The editor included a denial by Alabama State College officials that they had padlocked the dining center and starved students.

Firestorm of protest

Jenkins's report on the ad ignited a firestorm of protest among officials and others in Montgomery. They fiercely resented the northern news media's reports on the civil rights issue. Many southerners believed the issue was a matter that could best be handled by local officials. Grover Hall Jr., Jenkins's boss and editor-in-chief of the *Alabama Journal*'s sister paper, the *Montgomery Advertiser*, shared that view. When he read Jenkins's article, "[H]e came roaring out of his office . . . demanding to see this scurrilous ad," Jenkins recalled later. Infuriated, Hall wrote a scathing editorial in the following day's paper titled "Lies, lies, lies." In it, according to Jenkins, he "invited everyone in Alabama to sue the *New York Times*."

Several people took up Hall's challenge, with L. B. Sullivan leading the charge. Sullivan was a Montgomery

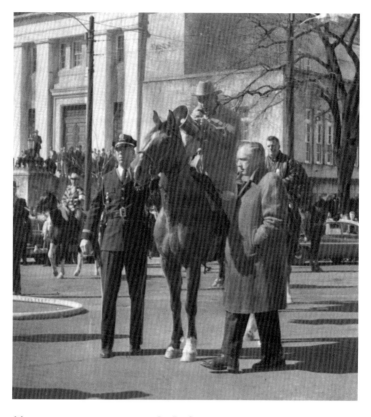

MONTGOMERY COMMISSIONER L. B. SULLIVAN, ON RIGHT, ACCOMPANIES POLICE OFFICERS AS THEY ATTEMPT TO DISPERSE CIVIL RIGHTS ACTIVISTS IN MONTGOMERY, ALABAMA, IN 1961.

official and the city's police commissioner. In that post, he supervised the police chief and the police force. He claimed that the ad appearing in the *New York Times* defamed him when it described "criminal police action" against college students as they sang on the steps of the Alabama capitol. The ad's statement that police "ringed the campus by truckloads armed with shotguns and tear gas" and that the dining hall was "padlocked to starve the students into submission" further defamed him, Sullivan charged. He also said that the ad led readers to believe that police—under his direction—were responsible for bombing King's home, assaulting him, and arresting him seven times. Even though the ad never mentioned Sullivan by name, he contended that as Montgomery's police commissioner, he would be blamed for any bad behavior by the police. The ad, he said, subjected him to "contempt, indignation, and ridicule."

In Southern culture, people placed a high value on reputation and polite behavior. In the previous century, men who believed their reputations had been sullied fought duels to reclaim their honor. The states' strict libel laws were passed to avoid duels and allow people to settle matters in court. These laws reinforced polite behavior and speech. Such laws aimed to maintain harmony and keep discourse on a high plane—no insults, no innuendoes, and no swear words. The laws also discouraged people from saying bad things about public officials, at least in public.

Every state had its own regulations concerning libel. Libel refers to published (or broadcast) statements that most people would consider to be harmful to someone's reputation. Under Alabama law, if those being sued for libel could prove that what they said was true, charges would be dropped. But if even one part of the statement could not be proved, the libel charge would stand. In the case of news stories, proving that every detail was true could be a challenge. Even if everything in the article were true, proving it in a court of law was often impossible. Many stories used testimony from unidentified sources unwilling to reveal themselves or eyewitnesses who did not want to testify. Reporters might have misspelled a street name or misidentified a source. Any error, no matter how insignificant, could eliminate the ability of a newspaper to use the truth defense.

DemanDs For retraction

In Alabama, before filing a libel suit, a public official had to demand a public retraction of the offensive words. If no retraction was published, the official could file suit. Following the requirements of the law, Sullivan wrote a letter to the *New York Times* demanding that the newspaper retract the claims made in the advertisement. He also demanded similar retractions from the Reverend Ralph D. Abernathy, the Reverend Fred L. Shuttlesworth, the Reverend S. S. Seay Sr., and the Reverend J. E. Lowery, who had been listed as supporting the ad's fund-raising appeal. The four black ministers were the only ones on the list who lived and worked in Alabama. State courts decided libel cases unless they involved parties from different states. Sullivan's lawyers included the ministers in the suit to strengthen the claim that the libel suit was a state case and that federal courts had no jurisdiction. They claimed the *Times* did business in the state because it sold 394 newspapers there.

The four ministers did not respond to Sullivan's letter. They claimed they had never heard of the ad before receiving the police commissioner's note and had not given permission for their names to be used in connection with the fund-raising appeal.

Several other Montgomery officials, including Alabama Governor John Patterson, claimed the ad had defamed them. Governor Patterson charged that the ad had accused him of "grave misconduct and . . . improper actions and omissions as Governor of Alabama and Ex-Officio Chairman of the State Board of Education of Alabama." Like Sullivan, he demanded a retraction from the *New York Times*.

The *New York Times* had a longstanding policy not to print retractions in response to libel charges. When the *Times* received Sullivan's note, the paper sent the police

ALABAMA GOVERNOR JOHN PATTERSON CHECKS A LAW BOOK IN HIS OFFICE.
ON THE WALL IS A PORTRAIT OF CONFEDERATE GENERAL JOSEPH WHEELER.
PATTERSON, WHO SERVED AS GOVERNOR FROM 1959 TO 1963, WAS AMONG SEV-
ERAL ALABAMA OFFICIALS WHO DEMANDED A RETRACTION FROM THE *NEW
YORK TIMES* FOR AN ADVERTISEMENT THE NEWSPAPER PRINTED IN 1960.

commissioner a letter questioning his claim that the ad libeled him personally. "We . . . are somewhat puzzled as to how you think the statements in any way reflect on you," the letter read. "You might, if you desire, let us know in what respect you claim that the statements in the advertisement reflect on you."

Sullivan made no reply. Instead, on April 19, he sued the newspaper and the four Alabama ministers for libel and asked for half a million dollars in damages.

The *Times* did print an apology to the governor in its May 16, 1960, edition. In part, the brief retraction read: "Since publication of the advertisement, the *Times* made an investigation and consistent with its policy of retracting and correcting any errors or misstatements which may appear in its columns, hereby retracts the two paragraphs complained of by the Governor. . . . To the extent that anyone can fairly conclude from the statements in the advertisement that any such charge [against the governor] was made, the *New York Times* hereby apologizes to the Honorable John Patterson therefor."

The two paragraphs referred to in the retraction contained the erroneous reports of police who "ringed" the campus of Alabama State College, the padlocked dining room, the crimes of "Southern violators," and the seven arrests of Dr. Martin Luther King Jr.

The secretary of the *New York Times* later testified in court why the paper decided to issue a retraction for the governor but not for Sullivan. By then, *Times* executive Harding Bancroft said, the newspaper had learned that some of the details of the ad were not true. The paper believed, he said, that the governor represented the state of Alabama and "[w]e didn't want anything that was published by the *Times* to be a reflection on the State of Alabama." Bancroft acknowledged that "the ad did refer to the action of the State authorities and the Board of

Education presumably of which the Governor is the ex-officio chairman."

The paper dismissed Sullivan's demand for a retraction, Bancroft said, because newspaper officials did not believe that "any of the language in [the ad] referred to Mr. Sullivan," since he had not been named in the ad.

Despite the publication of the retraction, the governor filed a libel suit in Montgomery County Circuit Court on May 30 against the *Times*, the four ministers, and Dr. King. He sought $1 million in damages. Three other Montgomery officials filed similar suits. Mayor Earl D. James, city commissioner Frank Parks, and former commissioner Clyde Sellers all sued the *Times* and the four ministers. Each suit asked for damages of $500,000.

TWO
THE BATTLE FOR CIVIL RIGHTS

AS THE reports OF protests and violence increased, the eyes of the nation focused on the South and the raging battle for equal rights for black citizens. In Montgomery, Alabama, where city officials had filed suit against the *New York Times*, protests had brought unwanted publicity to the city for several years.

Montgomery had been the site of one of the movement's earliest triumphs—the bus boycott begun in December 1955 after a black woman, Rosa Parks, refused to go to the back of the bus. The success of the protest catapulted its dynamic, twenty-six-year-old leader, Martin Luther King Jr., to national fame. The boycott, which lasted for 381 days, led to the desegregation of Montgomery buses in 1956. That same year, the U.S. Supreme Court, under Chief Justice Earl Warren, ruled that segregation on public buses was unconstitutional in the case of *Browder* v. *Gayle*.

In 1957, King became the first president of the newly formed Southern Christian Leadership Conference (SCLC). The group, founded by ministers, labor leaders, community activists, and lawyers, aimed to end segregation throughout the South.

As the movement's most visible leader, King soon came under attack by those who opposed integration. In 1956, enemies had bombed the King family's house. The

ROSA PARKS WALKS DOWN A STREET IN MONTGOMERY IN DECEMBER 1956 AFTER THE U.S. SUPREME COURT ISSUED A RULING THAT OUTLAWED SEGREGATION ON THE CITY'S BUSES. PARKS'S REFUSAL TO GIVE UP HER SEAT IN THE FRONT OF THE BUS SPARKED A CITYWIDE BOYCOTT OF THE BUS SYSTEM.

following year a second bomb, unexploded, was found on the Kings' front porch.

KING ARRESTED

Some southern officials opposed to King's policies used their power to harass the civil rights leader. Police arrested King several times on minor charges: driving five miles over the speed limit, trespassing during demonstrations, loitering. In early 1960, Alabama Governor John Patterson told state officials to arrest King on charges that he lied on his state income tax returns.

According to state officials, King had taken money raised for SCLC for his own use and had not reported it as personal income. The perjury charge carried with it a possible ten-year jail sentence.

King had recently moved to Atlanta, Georgia, to preach at his father's church and establish that city as headquarters for the desegregation campaign. On February 17, after an Alabama grand jury indicted King, police in Atlanta arrested him at the request of Alabama officials. He returned to Alabama to face trial. It was the first time in Alabama's history that perjury charges had been filed against someone for lying on an income tax return. The Montgomery grand jury accused King of "falsely, willfully and corruptly" filing an income tax return that listed his taxable income as $9,150. According to the state, King should have declared income of more than $16,000.

Newspaper reports on the case revealed that King had paid income tax on almost $27,000 of the money under dispute before police filed charges against him. A month after that report, the *Times* published the ad seeking funds for Dr. King's defense.

As King fought the charges against him, black students (and whites who supported them) reclaimed the nation's attention with sit-in protests at Alabama's public lunch counters and other facilities that banned blacks. Americans watched transfixed by news reports and television images of screaming white southerners who dumped plates of food on students' heads as they sat quietly waiting for service.

King's legal difficulties did little to silence him. He served as an adviser to students organizing the sit-ins and their newly formed Student Nonviolent Coordinating Committee (SNCC). On March 10, the *New York Times* reported that Dr. King had asked President Eisenhower to

DR. MARTIN LUTHER KING JR. HUGS HIS SON, MARTY, WHILE HIS WIFE, CORETTA, AND DAUGHTER, YOKI, GREET HIM. KING'S WORK TO PROMOTE CIVIL RIGHTS—AND DETENTION IN JAIL AS A RESULT OF HIS EFFORTS—OFTEN KEPT HIM APART FROM HIS FAMILY.

intervene in the South. The president, he said, should stop police "terror" directed at peaceful protesters during the Montgomery demonstrations. In April, King called on Americans everywhere to boycott businesses that practiced segregation.

Growing Sympathy for Civil Rights Movement

Publicity about the protests, the resulting violence against demonstrators, and the stirring words of King and others helped win support for the civil rights campaign outside

U.S. SENATOR LYNDON B. JOHNSON, DEMOCRAT FROM TEXAS AND SENATE MAJORITY LEADER, MAKES A POINT DURING A PRESS CONFERENCE IN 1955. JOHNSON PLAYED A LEADING ROLE IN WINNING PASSAGE OF THE CIVIL RIGHTS ACT OF 1960.

the South. As one writer noted in a letter to the *Times* editor, "Through sit-in demonstrations these courageous young people have made countless Americans understand that equality and justice are not abstractions, but as elementary as food and drink."

Senator Lyndon B. Johnson and others used the growing sympathy to push through a civil rights bill in 1960. Although the compromise version of the bill offered little to civil rights supporters, it did create a Civil Rights Commission and provided fines for anyone interfering with a citizen's attempt to vote.

The Montgomery perjury trial against Dr. King got under way in May. During the trial, King testified that not all the deposits to his bank account could be counted as income. The state auditor had recorded taxes on transfers of funds, repayments of loans, reimbursements for expenses, and other nontaxable items, according to King. King's lawyer accused the state of using "fraudulent techniques" and a "mathematical trick" to manufacture the charges against his client. The state's attorney accused King of "just plain lying." But the state's circuit solicitor said he did not expect any federal charges to be filed against King even though the federal government usually handled tax cases. Jurors had to sift through more than 1,400 pieces of evidence in the trial.

On May 28, 1960, after deliberating for only three hours and forty-five minutes, a jury of twelve white men acquitted King of the first of two perjury charges. King was cleared of another charge later that July. The verdict, King noted after the trial, was "very significant," not because he was acquitted but "because it offers a ray of hope for justice and understanding in the South."

The story covering King's acquittal ran on the front page of the *New York Times*. It was written by United Press International, since *Times* reporters had been ordered to stay out of Alabama to avoid getting served with papers on new suits. The *Times* also wanted to bolster its claims that the newspaper did not do business in the state and therefore the libel trials should go to federal court.

The fight for civil rights had been foremost in the

REPORTER BILL COOK, LEFT, INTERVIEWS FREEDOM RIDERS JIMMY
McDONALD, RIGHT, AND JAMES PECK, CENTER. THE TWO MEN WERE BEATEN
DURING A CIVIL RIGHTS DEMONSTRATION IN BIRMINGHAM IN 1961.

minds of those who had placed the fund-raising ad in the
New York Times two months earlier. One goal—to assist
King in his defense—had been realized. But the ad's central role—one no one would have guessed earlier—was yet
to be played out. This time the battle involved another
kind of rights—free speech and freedom of the press. The
struggle over the ad would take the U.S. Supreme Court—
and the nation—on a new course. The impact of the decision arising from that struggle would be felt for decades
to come.

THree
TO COURT

MONTGOMERY OFFICIALS were not alone in their suits against the *New York Times*. Not long after the publication of the fund-raising ad, *Times* reporter Harrison Salisbury's first article in a series on the South's civil rights struggles appeared in the newspaper. Salisbury's story, "Fear and Hatred Grip Birmingham," triggered a flurry of libel suits from that Alabama city. In addition, a grand jury indicted Salisbury on forty-two counts of criminal libel. The charges carried a jail term of up to twenty-one years.

When added to the Montgomery suits, the damages sought from the *Times* by the officials totaled more than $6 million. The enormity of the claims threatened to bankrupt the newspaper. "In all the years I have practiced law, nothing had ever arisen that was more worrisome," Louis Loeb, chief attorney for the *Times*, admitted later. "Nothing scared me more than this litigation."

BEFOre JUDGe JONES

On July 26, lawyers for the *Times* gathered at the Montgomery County Circuit Court to argue their case. Judge Walter B. Jones sat before them. Jones, one of the state's leading legal figures, had earned a reputation as a dedicated segregationist. The son of a former Alabama governor who was also a judge, Jones had ordered the

CIRCUIT COURT JUDGE WALTER B. JONES, A WELL-KNOWN SEGREGATIONIST, PRESIDED OVER THE TRIAL INVOLVING L. B. SULLIVAN'S SUIT AGAINST THE *NEW YORK TIMES*.

National Association for the Advancement of Colored People (NAACP) to stop operations in Alabama. The judge fined the Alabama branch of the civil rights organization $100,000, ordered it to give its membership lists to the state, and shut it down from 1956 to 1964.

Jones gained momentary fame when a renegade delegate to the electoral college cast a vote for the judge instead of Adlai Stevenson, the candidate to whom he was pledged. Appointed judge in 1920, Jones had established a law school, served as president of the Alabama State Bar, and founded the *Alabama Lawyer*, the state bar's official publication. He was also a columnist for the *Montgomery Advertiser*. In his "Off the Bench" column, the judge had once described abolitionist John Brown as "one of the ugliest characters in American history." Jones, a state commander of the Sons of Confederate Veterans, once seated jurors wearing Confederate uniforms to celebrate the founding of the Confederacy.

The *New York Times* lawyers based their case on the argument that the newspaper was not an Alabama firm and therefore could not be tried for libel in a state court. They argued that the corporation had no offices, employees, or property in the state, and asked the judge to dismiss the charges. During two days of testimony, Sullivan's lawyers argued otherwise. They said that *Times* reporters covered events in the state and that the news-paper hired stringers to report on issues of national importance. They produced cancelled checks, newspaper articles, letters, and other records dating back four years. *Times* lawyer Louis Loeb compared the paper's relation-ship with stringers (reporters working for local papers) to that of an out-of-state company that hired a detective to investigate a situation in Alabama. That did not make the company—or the *Times*—an Alabama business, the lawyers argued.

The testimony sparked several testy exchanges between Birmingham lawyer T. Eric Embry, representing the *Times*, and M. Roland Nachman Jr., Sullivan's lawyer. Embry objected that the court should be concerned only with the newspaper's current status. "Your Honor," he protested, "if you are going to allow these people to go all the way back to the birth of Christ—." Judge Jones, how-ever, overruled almost all of Embry's frequent objections.

In Sullivan's other libel suit, the four ministers testi-fied that they had never approved the use of their names in the ad. They asked the judge to dismiss the case against them.

On August 5, 1960, Judge Jones ruled that the *Times* did business in Alabama and thus could be sued for libel in state courts. The *Times* filed six separate motions

LOUIS LOEB, CHIEF ATTORNEY FOR THE *TIMES*, REPRESENTED THE NEWSPAPER AGAINST COMMISSIONER SULLIVAN'S SUIT IN CIRCUIT COURT.

appealing the ruling, but the judge denied them all. He also denied the ministers' request for a dismissal. Judge Jones would oversee trials in both suits.

SEGREGATED COURTROOM

The trial in the two cases began on November 1. Judge Jones's courtroom itself served as a symbol of the civil rights battle that had been featured in the disputed ad. The judge required strict segregation in the room, with blacks seated on one side and whites on the other. Before the trial even began, Jones announced that he considered the Fourteenth Amendment "a pariah and an outcast" if lawyers were going to use it to instruct him on how to run his courtroom. He claimed the "right and power to direct [and segregate] the seating of spectators in the courtroom."

For three days the jurors—twelve white men—heard testimony from local officials, *Times* representatives, and others. Since the judge had already struck down their major argument, the *Times* lawyers shifted their strategy. The ad, they argued, had not even mentioned Sullivan by name. The ad's accounts of the bombing of Martin Luther King Jr.'s home and of school officials' treatment of students clearly did not refer to the police commissioner. Several *Times* employees also contended that the newspaper had printed the ad in good faith and had not known that some of the details had been false. Even with the errors in the ad, *Times* official Harding Bancroft told the jury that he believed the ad had been "substantially correct."

During testimony, Sullivan said he believed the ad was directed at him, in particular the portions that mentioned the police. "As Commissioner of Public Affairs, it is part of my duty to supervise the Police Department and I certainly feel like it is associated with me when it describes police activities," he told the court. The untrue description of "truckloads of police" and other scenarios in the ad damaged his reputation, he said. Such statements, Sullivan claimed, "reflect upon my ability and integrity."

Six local men, including *Montgomery Advertiser* editor Grover Hall Jr., confirmed that they believed the ad referred to Sullivan. However, all the witnesses said they did not believe the accounts and did not think any less of Sullivan because of the ad. None could provide any examples of injury to the police commissioner caused by the ad. Four of the witnesses admitted they had not even seen the ad until Sullivan's lawyer showed it to them.

In his statement to the jury at the conclusion of the trial, Judge Jones said that the ad was so defamatory that it could be considered libelous without any further evidence, a legal circumstance known as libel *per se*. In such cases, plaintiffs do not have to prove that they were actually injured in order to collect damages. He noted that defendants could protect themselves from libel suits by proving only that they had published the truth. But that defense could not be used in this case, since both sides acknowledged that some of the ad's accounts were not true. The judge also told the jury that Sullivan did not have to be named in the ad as long as he could prove that the words were directed at him. That left the jury with the duty to decide if the *Times* had published the ad, if it had referred to L. B. Sullivan, and if so, whether he should receive damages.

Regarding the black ministers' case, Judge Jones said that even if the four had not given permission for their names to be used in the ad, they could still be found guilty of libel if they agreed with the ad after it was published. That was the argument Sullivan's lawyers had used. It would be up to the jury to determine whether to hold the ministers responsible.

GUILTY VerDICTS

Two hours later, the jury returned to the courtroom with its verdict. Agreeing that the ad libeled the police commissioner, the jurors awarded Sullivan the full $500,000 he had requested. They found the four ministers guilty as well. At the time it was the largest libel award in the state.

Sullivan's success was the first in a string of decisions against the *Times*. Soon after, another jury awarded Montgomery's mayor, Earl D. James, a half-million dollar settlement. Governor Patterson sued for double that amount—one million dollars—and won it. Two other half-million-dollar lawsuits waited for court rulings.

Soon after the judgment was filed, the *New York Times* appealed the verdict. Denied a new trial, the *Times* sought a hearing in the state's supreme court.

THrOuGH THe cOurT SYSTem

First Stop: State Court
Almost all cases (about 95 percent) start in state courts. These courts go by various names, depending on the state in which they operate: circuit, district, municipal, county, or superior. The case is tried and decided by a judge, a panel of judges, or a jury.

The side that loses can then appeal to the next level.

First Stop: Federal Court
U.S. DISTRICT COURT—About 5 percent of cases begin their journey in federal court. Most of these cases concern federal laws, the U.S. Constitution, or disputes that involve two or more states. They are heard in one of the ninety-four U.S. district courts in the nation.
U.S. COURT OF INTERNATIONAL TRADE—Federal court cases involving international trade appear in the U.S. Court of International Trade.
U.S. CLAIMS COURT—The U.S. Claims Court hears federal cases that involve more than $10,000, Indian claims, and some disputes with government contractors.

The loser in federal court can appeal to the next level.

Appeals: State Cases
Forty states have appeals courts that hear cases that have come from the state courts. In states without an appeals court, the case goes directly to the state supreme court.

Appeals: Federal Cases
U.S. CIRCUIT COURT—Cases appealed from U.S. district courts go to U.S. circuit courts of appeals. There are twelve circuit courts that handle cases from throughout the

nation. Each district court and every state and territory are assigned to one of the twelve circuits. Appeals in a few state cases—those that deal with rights guaranteed by the U.S. Constitution—are also heard in this court.

U.S. COURT OF APPEALS—Cases appealed from the U.S. Court of International Trade and the U.S. Claims Court are heard by the U.S. Court of Appeals for the Federal Circuit. Among the cases heard in this court are those involving patents and minor claims against the federal government.

Further Appeals: State Supreme Court

Cases appealed from state appeals courts go to the highest courts in the state—usually called supreme court. In New York, the state's highest court is called the court of appeals. Most state cases do not go beyond this point.

Final Appeals: U.S. Supreme Court

The U.S. Supreme Court is the highest court in the country. Its decision on a case is the final word. The Court decides issues that can affect every person in the nation. It has decided cases on slavery, abortion, school segregation, and many other important issues.

The Court selects the cases it will hear—usually around one hundred each year. Four of the nine justices must vote to consider a case in order for it to be heard. Almost all cases have been appealed from the lower courts (either state or federal).

Most people seeking a decision from the Court submit a petition for *certiorari*. Certiorari means that the case will be moved from a lower court to a higher court for review. The Court receives about nine thousand of these requests annually. The petition outlines the case and gives reasons why the Court should review it.

In rare cases, for example *New York Times* v. *United States*, an issue must be decided immediately. When such a case is of national importance, the Court allows it to bypass the usual lower court system and hears the case directly.

To win a spot on the Court's docket, a case must fall within one of the following categories:

- Disputes between states and the federal government or between two or more states. The Court also reviews cases involving ambassadors, consuls, and foreign ministers.

- Appeals from state courts that have ruled on a federal question.

- Appeals from federal appeals courts (about two-thirds of all requests fall into this category).

The Reverend Ralph Abernathy was one of four Southern ministers to be named in Commissioner L. B. Sullivan's suit.

While the ruling caused concern among *Times* officials and advocates of a free press, the four black ministers came under immediate and personal attack. The Reverend Ralph Abernathy was forced to sell his share in a plot of land in the western part of the state to help pay his part of the damages. The state put liens on the cars of two of the ministers and auctioned Abernathy's five-year-old Buick for four hundred dollars. When the ministers did not attend a hearing on the appeal, Judge Jones ruled that they would not be allowed to participate in a new trial. That decision was overturned, however, and their case remained tied to that of the *Times*. The two cases would eventually travel together to the U.S. Supreme Court.

four
FREEDOM OF THE PRESS

LONG BEFORE THE UNITED STATES of America stood as an independent nation, its people recognized the importance of a free press. The early colonists brought printing presses to America and a distaste for government censorship. The colonies' first newspaper, *Publick Occurrences Both Forreign and Domestick*, began and ended its career with a blistering attack on Boston's colonial officials on September 25, 1690. Enraged by publisher Benjamin Harris's articles, the colonial government closed the paper down after only one edition. The government took the paper to task for publishing "sundry doubtful and uncertain Reports" and suppressed any further editions. Colonial officials also banned publishers from producing "anything in print" without first obtaining permission from the government.

Despite that inauspicious beginning, newspapers prospered. Boston postmaster John Campbell began publishing the nation's first successful newspaper in 1704. Unlike its predecessor, Campbell's *Boston News-Letter* was published with the permission of the colonial government, a fact noted on the front page. The newspaper carried foreign, regional, and local news but shied away from reports critical of the colonial administration. Campbell continued to operate the paper after leaving the postmaster position. His successor, William Brooker,

PUBLICK OCCURRENCES BOTH FORREIGN AND DOMESTICK WAS THE FIRST NEWSPAPER TO BE PRINTED IN BRITAIN'S AMERICAN COLONIES.

founded a rival paper, the *Boston Gazette*, in 1719, which also reported favorably on the current administration. As rivals, however, the two papers began to report on opposite sides of issues affecting the colonists. The governor and local representatives to the assembly, the governing body of the Massachusetts colony, disagreed on a number of issues. Both sides used the two newspapers to air their political views.

COLONISTS CHALLENGE CONTROL OF PRESS

Although the ruling British governors held authority over printing and could ban anything they viewed as "obnoxious," colonists continually challenged this authority. They produced pamphlets and flyers that targeted political and religious leaders, including England's king and colonial leaders.

In March 1721 Samuel Shute, colonial governor of Massachusetts, tried to reassert control over printing. He proposed a law that would have required all printers to obtain a license from the governor before publishing anything. The assembly members objected, saying such a license would create "innumerable inconveniences and danger" for Massachusetts colonists. They preferred to punish publishers after they printed objectionable materials rather than requiring publishers to get permission to print in advance.

Shute then pushed for a law to prevent libelous material from being published and to punish those who printed such material. The governor's council approved the bill, but the colony's representatives voted against it. Both Boston newspapers and various flyers and pamphlets reported the episode. The defeat of Shute's bill ended English efforts to license the Massachusetts press.

Soon newspapers began to appear in the other

COLONIAL OFFICIALS BURN COPIES OF JOHN PETER ZENGER'S NEWSPAPER.

colonies as well. These publications, printed weekly or daily, served to unite the communities and keep colonists informed on a wide range of topics. They reported the names and cargo of ships coming to port, published news accounts from the foreign press, printed official government reports, and ran advertisements for everything from elixirs to land.

The newspapers also continued to be a thorn in the

government's side. In 1733 John Peter Zenger criticized the colonial governor in his *New York Weekly Journal*. The government jailed him on libel charges, even though the information he published had been true. At Zenger's trial, his lawyers appealed to the jury that the truth should not be considered libel. The jurors ruled in Zenger's favor, in a case that served as a landmark for a free press in America.

During the years leading up to the American Revolution, printed flyers and underground newspapers played a major role in spreading discontent with English rule. The Stamp Act of 1765, which taxed all printed materials in the colonies, sparked a flurry of pamphlets and leaflets—printed by Boston patriot Samuel Adams, among others—that ultimately forced the English to repeal the onerous tax. "Your Press has sounded the alarm. . . . It has pointed to this people their danger and their remedy," a triumphant Adams said, commenting on the important role the press had played in the protest.

Paine's Pamphlet Ignites War

Firebrand Thomas Paine used his writing skills to help ignite the passions of his countrymen in the months leading up to the Revolutionary War. He was the first to write about uniting the colonies and separating from England. *Common Sense*, published in 1776, urged Americans to cut ties with England: "Every thing that is right or natural pleads for separation. The blood of the slain, the weeping voice of nature cries, *'TIS TIME TO PART*." This publication, called "the first cry for national life," inspired those rebelling against England's control and helped launch the resistance that became the American Revolution. "No pamphlet, no book, ever kindled such a sudden conflagration," said noted nineteenth-century orator Robert G. Ingersoll about Paine's *Common Sense*.

After the war, America's early leaders worked to

develop a system of government that would protect its people from abuse of power. Thomas Jefferson, who had written the Declaration of Independence, realized the importance of freedom of the press in protecting against a too-powerful government. Although he was serving as minister to France in 1787 when the Constitution was being written, his letters influenced the new leaders' decisions. "Our liberty," Jefferson wrote in one letter, "depends on the freedom of the press, and that cannot be limited without being lost."

During negotiations over the U.S. Constitution, some founders pushed for the addition of a list of rights that would spell out the freedoms guaranteed the people. Ten of these amendments, called the Bill of Rights, became part of the Constitution when they were ratified in 1791. The First Amendment specifically guaranteed the freedom of the press. The fact that it was included in the first of the ten amendments indicates the importance of a free press to early American leaders.

SEDITION ACTS

Even the First Amendment guarantee of freedom of the press did not stop government officials from trying to censor printing that criticized their activities. Only seven years after the Bill of Rights was ratified, the U.S. Congress passed a sweeping law aimed at silencing critics. The Sedition Act of 1798 made it a crime to publish "any false, scandalous and malicious writings" against the government, Congress, or the president. Those convicted under the law faced up to five years in prison and fines of up to $5,000 (equal to more than $100,000 today). Supporters claimed that the law was necessary to protect the nation against threats from France after that country's revolution. But the law's proponents also hoped the law, and other repressive acts passed at the same time, would destroy Thomas Jefferson and his party, which had voiced support for the French Revolution.

Shortly after the bill became law, police arrested more than a dozen letter writers, editors, and others and charged them with writing seditious material. Some newspapers were forced to close down; others stopped printing anything critical of Adams or the government. The first to be arrested, Matthew Lyon, represented Vermont in the U.S. House of Representatives. A newspaper had published his letter opposing war with France and accusing President Adams of being "swallowed up in a continued grasp of power." Lyon argued that he had merely expressed his political views, but the jury—all supporters of Adams—found him guilty of writing with "bad intent." The judge—also an Adams supporter—fined the congressman $1,000 and imposed a four-month jail sentence. While Lyon spent the winter in jail, his constituents voted him into office for another term. After his release, he returned to Congress to the cheers of his supporters.

The police actions against Lyon and others enraged the public and helped elect Thomas Jefferson president in 1800. The law expired on March 3, 1801, the last day of Adams's presidency. Once in office, Jefferson pardoned those convicted under the act. Four decades later, in 1840, Congress passed a law to reimburse those forced to pay fines under the Sedition Act.

In the early 1900s, when another war threatened, the government once again sought to silence critics. Congress passed a new Sedition Act in 1918 in response to fears that criticism would weaken America's position during World War I. The new law, passed as an amendment to the Espionage Act of 1917, barred Americans from using "profane, scurrilous, or abusive language about the form of government . . . the Constitution . . . or the flag of the United States, or the uniform of the Army and Navy."

Under the law's provisions, the government banned several books, newspapers, and journals. Police also arrested critics of the administration, particularly those who opposed the war. Eugene V. Debs, a socialist who had run for president in 1912, was arrested after speaking out against the war at a 1918 rally. The U.S. Supreme Court upheld his conviction and ten-year jail sentence, but President Warren G. Harding pardoned him in 1921.

The high court upheld the Espionage Act and the Sedition Act in another case, *Schenck* v. *United States*, in 1919. Charles T. Schenck had distributed a pamphlet during World War I that claimed the military draft was illegal. He sent the pamphlets to men who had been drafted into the military. Lower courts found him guilty of violating the Espionage Act. The Supreme Court upheld Schenck's conviction.

In his decision for the Court, Justice Oliver Wendell Holmes set limits on free speech. He wrote that Congress could ban words that created "a clear and present danger" to the nation. Words that might be allowed during peacetime, Holmes reasoned, could interfere with a nation's wartime efforts. In that case, he said, the Constitution offered no protection.

Congress repealed the Sedition Act in 1920, but the *Schenck* decision stood as the rule of law used to judge other free speech cases. Later rulings, however, would make it more difficult to ban written material.

RULING STRIKES DOWN CENSORSHIP

Another major ruling, one that would play a role in *Sullivan* and other freedom of the press cases, came in 1931 in *Near* v. *Minnesota*. The case concerned a series of articles published in 1927 by Jay M. Near in his weekly newspaper, *The Saturday Press*. The articles reported that "Jewish gangsters" oversaw gambling, bootlegging, and racketeering operations in Minneapolis. The newspaper also named city officials who, the paper claimed, allowed the operations to run without police interference.

The county attorney charged Near with breaking the state law banning publication of "a malicious, scandalous and defamatory newspaper, magazine or other period- ical." The law allowed such news accounts to be published only if they could be proved true and only if they were published "with good motives and for justifiable ends." Otherwise, they were considered a public nuisance and were banned.

When his case reached the U.S. Supreme Court, Near claimed the law violated the Constitution's guarantee of freedom of the press. In a strongly worded decision, Chief Justice Charles Evans Hughes struck down the Minnesota law and reconfirmed the important role the press played in a democracy. He noted that the United States might be "miserable colonies, groaning under a foreign yoke" if the Sedition Act of 1798 had still been in force. Instead, he said, the country had become a "free and independent nation," in large part because of a free press. Democracy depended on a free press to uncover corruption and gov- ernmental abuses.

Hughes concluded with a ringing endorsement of freedom of the press: "To the press alone, chequered as it is with abuses, the world is indebted for all the triumphs which have been gained by reason and humanity over error and oppression."

As important as the *Near* decision was in protecting a free press, it dealt mainly with censorship and the gov- ernment's efforts to prevent certain things from being printed. That was not allowed, under the *Near* ruling, except in extraordinary circumstances during war or other national crisis. Once objectionable words had been printed, however, the decision allowed for "punishment"

for libel. Chief Justice Hughes's majority opinion explic-
itly approved libel laws:

> [P]unishment for the abuse of the liberty
> accorded the press is essential to the protection of
> the public, and . . . the common law rules that sub-
> ject the libeler to responsibility for the public
> offense, as well as for the private injury, are not
> abolished by the protection extended in our con-
> stitutions. . . . For whatever wrong the appellant
> has committed or may commit, by his publica-
> tions, the state appropriately affords both public
> and private redress by its libel laws.

NO ProTecTIONS FOr LIBeL

A whole category of words—those considered libelous—lay
outside the protection of the Constitution, at least as far as
the Supreme Court was concerned.

Public officials had long objected to libelous attacks in
the press. Francis Hopkinson, who signed the Declaration
of Independence, defended a free press—as long as it did
not malign the institutions he held dear.

> [W]hen this privilege is manifestly abused, and
> the press becomes an engine for sowing the most
> dangerous dissensions, for spreading false
> alarms, and undermining the very foundations of
> government, ought not that government upon the
> plain principles of self-preservation to silence by
> its own authority such a daring violator of its
> peace, and tear from its bosom the serpent that
> would sting it to death?

Until the *Sullivan* case, the Court left libel cases in the
hands of state courts. During its history, the Court had

turned down requests to review forty-four libel cases. Only three such cases had won hearings before the high court. Two of those cases involved executives working for the president. The Court granted them immunity from libel suits that involved statements made while they were on the job. In the third case, the Court ruled that a television station could not be sued for libel for statements made by political candidates given equal time on air to discuss their views.

Each state had its own laws governing libel. In most (but not all) states, truth was an acceptable defense against libel. But unlike criminal cases in which the accuser had to prove the truth of the charge, in libel cases the situation was reversed. The person or publisher accused of libel had to prove that the objectionable statements were true. Claims that the libel laws violated the First Amendment got nowhere.

In addition to the *Near* decision, the Supreme Court noted in several other cases that the First Amendment did not protect certain types of speech from prosecution. The Court upheld this view in a 1942 case, *Chaplinsky* v. *New Hampshire*. The case arose after Walter Chaplinsky, a member of the Jehovah's Witnesses, distributed pamphlets about his religion near City Hall in Rochester, New Hampshire. Police responded when a crowd objecting to Chaplinsky's pamphlet gathered and became rowdy. A marshal called to the scene did not arrest the troublemakers but instead escorted Chaplinsky to the police station. An angry Chaplinsky called the marshal a racketeer and a fascist. Police arrested him and charged him under the city's law that made it illegal for people to address others in public by "any offensive or derisive name."

The Supreme Court affirmed Chaplinsky's conviction. Justice Frank Murphy, writing for the Court, stated that Chaplinsky's "fighting words" were among the few types of speech not protected by the First Amendment. There were, Murphy wrote:

> certain well-defined and narrowly limited classes of speech, the prevention and punishment of which have never been thought to raise any Constitutional problem. These include the lewd and obscene, the profane, the libelous, and the insulting or "fighting" words—those which by their very utterance inflict injury or tend to incite an immediate breach of the peace.

The Court removed libel from the protections of the First Amendment in a 1952 case. The case, *Beauharnais* v. *Illinois*, involved a man found guilty of libeling a group of people after he distributed racist pamphlets on the streets of Chicago. Justice Felix Frankfurter's majority opinion noted that prosecutors did not even have to prove libelous statements were a "clear and present danger," the test Justice Holmes had offered in judging whether speech should be banned:

> Libelous utterances not being within the area of constitutionally protected speech, it is unnecessary, either for us or for the State courts, to consider the issues behind the phrase "clear and present danger." Certainly no one would contend that obscene speech, for example, may be punished only upon a showing of such circumstances. Libel, as we have seen, is in the same class.

Frankfurter did leave a small opening for those who might claim their rights had been violated by overzealous libel laws. The Court, he noted, still had the power "to nullify action which encroaches on freedom of utterance

U.S. Supreme Court Justice Felix Frankfurter wrote the decision in a 1952 Illinois case that removed libel from the protections of the First Amendment.

under the guise of punishing libel." He added, "Of course discussion cannot be denied and the right, as well as the duty, of criticism must not be stifled."

A 1961 case, *Konigsberg* v. *State Bar of California*, also touched on questions of free speech. State bar examiners had denied Raphael Konigsberg's application to become a lawyer in California after he refused to answer questions about membership in the Communist Party. The Supreme

Court ruled that the bar examiners had not violated Konigsberg's First Amendment rights. In that decision, Justice John M. Harlan wrote that "certain forms of speech, or speech in certain contexts, has been considered outside the scope of constitutional protection." Sullivan's lawyers used that statement and the *Beauharnais* ruling to bolster their claim that the First Amendment did not apply to the libelous ad in the *Times*.

Free speech protections expanded

While the few Court cases that touched on libel provided little to support the *Times*'s position, decisions in related areas offered more hope. During the 1940s and 1950s, the Court began to ease some of the restrictions on speech, union activities, and other forms of expression. A 1940s case, *Terminiello* v. *Chicago*, strengthened the rights of speakers whose words caused disturbances among listeners. In that decision, Justice William O. Douglas, a noted free-speech advocate, wrote that "[t]he vitality of civil and political institutions in our society depends on free discussion." Speech, he said, should be restricted only when the disturbance it caused was "likely to produce a clear and present danger of a serious substantive evil." Creating "public inconvenience, annoyance, or unrest," according to Justice Douglas, should not be grounds to ban speech or expression. "[A] function of free speech under our system of government is to invite dispute," the justice wrote. "It may indeed best serve its high purpose when it induces a condition of unrest, creates dissatisfaction with conditions as they are, or even stirs people to anger."

A 1957 ruling, *Roth* v. *United States*, rejected First Amendment arguments for obscenity. The case involved a New York bookseller, Samuel Roth, convicted of sending obscene circulars and a book through the mail. The Court joined the *Roth* case to *Alberts* v. *California*, the case of a California man convicted of similar charges when he mailed obscene books and advertisements. In writing the Court's 6 to 3 decision, Justice Brennan concluded: "We hold that obscenity is not within the area of constitutionally protected speech or press."

The *Roth* case placed obscenity, along with libel, commercial speech, and "fighting words," among the four areas of speech not protected under the First Amendment. But by accepting the *Roth* case, the Court at least had agreed to review the laws governing obscenity. Although the Court had ruled against Roth, the justices had reiterated their support of free speech and its important role in government by the people. Brennan noted in the *Roth* opinion that the nation's founders had ensured freedom of speech and of the press "to assure unfettered interchange of ideas for the bringing about of political and social changes desired by the people." The *New York Times*'s lawyers would use that statement in defending the newspaper against Sullivan before the U.S. Supreme Court.

Until the passage of the Fourteenth Amendment in 1868, the Bill of Rights protected citizens' rights only when dealing with the federal government. States were free to set their own laws regarding citizens' treatment. The Fourteenth Amendment, however, barred states from abridging "the privileges or immunities of citizens" and required them to follow "due process" in their dealings with people. It also prohibited the states from denying anyone "the equal protection of the laws." The Supreme Court under Chief Justice Earl Warren adopted that principle—called incorporation—to force the states to comply with several controversial rulings, including school desegregation. Because of the incorporation precedent, the *Times*'s lawyers in the *Sullivan* case based their defense on both the First and the Fourteenth amendments.

THE FOURTEENTH AMENDMENT: ENSURING RIGHTS FOR ALL

Section. 1. All persons born or naturalized in the United States and subject to the jurisdiction thereof, are citizens of the United States and of the State wherein they reside. No State shall make or enforce any law which shall abridge the privileges or immunities of citizens of the United States; nor shall any State deprive any person of life, liberty, or property, without due process of law; nor deny to any person within its jurisdiction the equal protection of the laws.

Section. 2. Representatives shall be apportioned among the several States according to their respective numbers, counting the whole number of persons in each State, excluding Indians not taxed. But when the right to vote at any election for the choice of electors for President and Vice President of the United States, Representatives in Congress, the Executive and Judicial officers of a State, or the members of the Legislature thereof, is denied to any of the male inhabitants of such State, being twenty-one years of age, and citizens of the United States, or in any way abridged, except for participation in rebellion, or other crime, the basis of representation therein shall be reduced in the proportion which the number of such male citizens shall bear to the whole number of male citizens twenty-one years of age in such State.

Section. 3. No person shall be a Senator or Representative in Congress, or elector of President and Vice President, or hold any office, civil or military, under the United States, or under any State, who, having previously taken an oath, as a member of Congress, or as an officer of the United States, or as a member of any State legislature, or as an executive or judicial officer of any State, to support the Constitution of the United States, shall have engaged in insurrection or rebellion against the same, or given aid or comfort to the enemies thereof. But Congress may by a vote of two-thirds of each House, remove such disability.

Section. 4. The validity of the public debt of the United States, authorized by law, including debts incurred for payment of pensions and bounties for services in suppressing insurrection or rebellion, shall not be questioned. But neither the United States nor any State shall assume or pay any debt or obligation incurred in aid of insurrection or rebellion against the United States, or any claim for the loss or emancipation of any slave; but all such debts, obligations and claims shall be held illegal and void.

Section. 5. The Congress shall have power to enforce, by appropriate legislation, the provisions of this article.

The First Amendment bars the U.S. Congress from making any law that would establish a particular religion or prevent Americans from freely exercising their religion. It says nothing about what state legislatures can and cannot do.

For years the states used that loophole to pass laws that conflicted with First Amendment protections. In the 1845 case *Permoli* v. *Municipality No. 1 of City of New Orleans*, for example, the Supreme Court upheld Louisiana's argument that the First Amendment did not apply to them. Justice John Catron, writing for the majority, ruled: "The Constitution makes no provision for protecting the citizens of the respective states in their religious liberties; this is left to the state constitutions and laws."

After the Civil War, Congress sought to close that particular loophole with the passage of the Fourteenth Amendment. Whites in the South had used the loophole to deprive freed slaves of their rights as citizens. With the ratification of the amendment on July 28, 1868, former slaves and all others "born or naturalized in the United States" automatically became American citizens. As citizens, they could vote, own property, and engage in business.

The amendment also directed the states not to deprive anyone, citizen and noncitizen alike, of "life, liberty, or property, without due process of law"; nor the "equal protection of the laws." In addition, the amendment specifically forbade the states from limiting citizens' "privileges or immunities."

For decades after the amendment was passed, however, it offered little protection against state actions. The *Slaughterhouse Cases* set the stage for a conservative view of the amendment.

In March 1869 the Louisiana Legislature granted exclusive rights to the Crescent City Live-Stock Landing and Slaughter-House Company to run slaughterhouses in part of the state. Other slaughterhouse companies objected and filed suit. The U.S. Supreme Court heard the arguments in the suits—which became known as the *Slaughterhouse Cases*—in 1872 and 1873. The plaintiffs argued that the state had deprived them of their rights as citizens to earn a living, guaranteed under the Fourteenth Amendment. They also claimed the Louisiana law denied them "equal protection of the laws" and deprived them of liberty and property "without due process of law," in violation of the Fourteenth Amendment.

The Court ruled against the plaintiffs. In its April 14, 1873, decision, the Court decreed that the Fourteenth Amendment applied only to national rights. The amendment's protections did not extend to state contracts, state elections, or other matters overseen by the state, according to the Court. The ruling allowed states to control the civil rights of their citizens.

Over time, however, the Court began to apply the Fourteenth Amendment to protect citizens against wrongful actions by the states. Under this doctrine, the rights listed in the Bill of Rights are said to be *incorporated* by the Fourteenth Amendment. This doctrine has been referred to as "the second Bill of Rights" because it protected against unreasonable state power as the original ten amendments protected against federal abuses. Among other things, the policy played a key role in preserving Americans' religious liberties against state laws that favored certain religions.

One of the earliest cases in which the Court used the incorporation doctrine to limit a state's power was *Gitlow* v. *New York*. The case involved a socialist named Benjamin Gitlow, who was arrested after distributing copies of a paper urging people to strike and to take "revolutionary mass action." The state court convicted Gitlow of advocating the overthrow of the government. Gitlow appealed to the U.S. Supreme Court. In its decision, issued in 1925, the Court ruled against Gitlow because his actions endangered the state. Nevertheless, the Court asserted that the Fourteenth Amendment required states as well as Congress not to abridge the First Amendment's guarantee of free speech:

[W]e may and do assume that freedom of speech and of the press—which are protected by the First Amendment from abridgment by Congress—are among the fundamental personal rights and "liberties" protected by the due process clause of the Fourteenth Amendment from impairment by the States.

In their dissent, Justices Oliver Wendell Holmes and Louis Brandeis argued that Gitlow's diatribe presented no immediate danger to the government and should be protected under the Constitution's free speech guarantees. They, too, supported the doctrine that the Fourteenth Amendment protected free speech from state control.

During the 1930s and 1940s, the Supreme Court applied other First Amendment rights to the states. The Warren Court in the 1950s and 1960s made extensive use of the incorporation doctrine. With its focus on civil and individual rights, the Warren Court used the doctrine to order school desegregation, ban school prayers, and establish protections for criminal defendants. Later Courts have used the doctrine to strike down state laws banning abortion, to guarantee privacy rights, and to ensure other rights not specifically mentioned in the Constitution.

FIVE
MAKING THEIR CASE

AFTER LOSING IN Judge Walter B. Jones's court, *New York Times* officials hired Herbert Wechsler to argue their case. Wechsler had served as a law clerk to U.S. Supreme Court Justice Harlan Fiske Stone and was a respected law professor at Columbia. He would later go on to serve as director of the American Law Institute for more than twenty years. As an assistant attorney general during and after World War II, he developed guidelines for trying Nazi war criminals during the Nuremberg trials.

Wechsler believed that the lower court's ruling in *Sullivan* and state libel laws stood at odds with the First Amendment's guarantee of a free press. He convinced the *Times* that the defense should focus on constitutional issues. He used that argument as well as others when he filed the newspaper's appeal with the state supreme court.

Both the *Times* and the four ministers asked the appeals court to overturn Judge Jones's ruling. The ministers repeated their claim that they had never given permission for their names to be used in the ad and that they had nothing to do with its contents. Therefore, they argued, they should not be held responsible. The *Times* argued that the court should grant its appeal because:

• The newspaper was not an Alabama business and the case should not have been heard in state court.

HERBERT WECHSLER, A PROFESSOR AT COLUMBIA LAW SCHOOL, ARGUED THE CASE BEFORE THE U.S. SUPREME COURT FOR THE *NEW YORK TIMES*.

• The ad made no mention of Sullivan.
• Sullivan did not show that the ad had damaged his reputation or caused him harm.
• The paper published the ad in good faith and with no malice toward the commissioner (or anyone else).
• The judge should not have instructed the jury that the ad was libelous *per se* but should have

64

allowed jurors to decide for themselves whether the ad was libelous.
• The damages awarded to Sullivan ($500,000) were excessive.
• The judge's order abridged the freedom of the press, deprived the *Times* of its property without due process, and violated the First and Fourteenth Amendments to the Constitution.

This last argument, Wechsler believed, was the strongest and most important. But the Alabama Supreme Court rejected the constitutional claims and all of the other points raised by the *Times* and the ministers. On August 30, 1962, the court handed down its ruling upholding Judge Jones's opinion. Much of the lengthy opinion issued by the appeals court dealt with the *Times*'s claims that the paper was not an Alabama business. The state's high court took particular issue with Harding Bancroft's assertion that the ad had been "substantially correct." Such a statement in the face of all the evidence that the ad's statements were false, the court noted, revealed to the jury the *Times*'s "bad faith and maliciousness."

The court dismissed the constitutional claims in two sentences:

• The First Amendment of the U.S. Constitution does not protect libelous publications.
• The Fourteenth Amendment is directed against state action and not private action.

According to the appeals court, the Bill of Rights did not apply.

The verdict left the *Times* and the four ministers with a $500,000 debt to be paid to Commissioner Sullivan.

They decided to take their appeal to the next—and final—court, the U.S. Supreme Court.

Petitioning for a Supreme Court Hearing

Winning a spot on the U.S. Supreme Court's calendar can be even more daunting than arguing the case. At the time of the *Sullivan* appeal, the Court received more than 1,500 petitions for a hearing annually. During its October to June session, the Court heard only about 150 cases. Chances of being selected as one of the few cases were slim.

Wechsler had several reasons for believing that the Court would agree to hear the *Times*'s case. First, the case dealt with a federal constitutional issue. Second, libel laws had never been judged by the Court in light of the First Amendment guarantee of a free press. And finally, threatened libel cases could deter the press from doing its job and reporting on the civil rights battle that consumed the South and affected the entire nation.

In November 1962, the *Times* and the four ministers filed a petition for a writ of *certiorari* asking for a Supreme Court review. *Certiorari* is the Latin word for "to be informed of." If the Court grants a writ of *certiorari*, it orders the lower courts to turn over the records on the case so the higher court can "be informed" and review the proceedings.

During each session, the nine justices of the Supreme Court gather for weekly conferences to discuss upcoming appeals, review arguments already given, and decide which cases they will hear. For the Court to consider a case, four justices must vote to review it.

On January 7, 1963, the Supreme Court announced that it would hear the *Sullivan* case along with its companion case, *Abernathy et al.* v. *Sullivan*. Because the justices had no time left to hear cases during their current term, the lawyers in the *Sullivan* case would wait for a full year before appearing in court. Oral arguments in the case would be given on January 6, 1964 (for the *Times*) and January 7, 1964 (for Abernathy and the other three ministers).

The lawyers on both sides spent the next months preparing exhaustive reports on the two cases. In these reports, called briefs, the lawyers described the incidents leading to the suit, outlined the issues involved, discussed the lower court hearings, gave arguments that supported their view of things, and cited past Court decisions that bolstered their clients' interests. In addition to the briefs filed by lawyers for the *Times*, the ministers, and Sullivan, the Court allowed three other briefs to be submitted. These—called *amici curiae* ("friend of the court")—were filed by the *Washington Post*, the *Chicago Tribune*, and the American Civil Liberties Union. All argued that the lower court's decision should be reversed.

History weighs heavy on the Supreme Court. Tradition dictates who sits where, how the justices are addressed, even the words used to call the Court to order. The justices rely on past rulings or precedents—some reaching back a century ago or more—to guide them in their decisions. Lawyers cite previous cases to support their arguments. Only rarely does the Supreme Court overturn its own rulings. And rarely does the Court throw out practices that have been accepted and followed for years to forge new laws. The *Times*'s lawyer undertook an awesome task. He set out to convince the Court that libel laws, the sole responsibility of the states since the nation's founding, should now come under Court review.

THE *New York Times* Brief

Wechsler, in the ninety-five-page brief submitted to the Court, based his case on three main arguments:

1. The First Amendment did not allow libel laws to abridge the freedom of the press.
2. Even if the existing libel laws were ruled constitutional, the facts of the *Sullivan* case did not support the ruling or the "enormous" damages.
3. The state of Alabama did not have jurisdiction in the case.

Wechsler devoted twenty pages to his main argument that Alabama's libel law violated the First Amendment. The state's law, as interpreted by the lower courts, restricted protest and criticism of actions by public officials, according to the *Times*'s lawyer.

He acknowledged that the Court had in the past allowed libel judgments to stand. But he argued that none of the cases had supported suppressing criticism of government action.

Even in the *Beauharnais* case, in which the Court had stated that the First Amendment did not protect libelous statements, Justice Frankfurter had reiterated support for freedom of the press, Wechsler noted. He quoted Frankfurter's warning that the Court had the "authority to nullify action which encroaches on freedom of utterance under the guise of punishing libel." He added the justice's statements that "public men are, as it were, public property," and that "discussion cannot be denied and the right, as well as the duty, of criticism must not be stifled."

The "mere label" of libel should not prevent the Court from reviewing the state law to make certain it did not violate the First Amendment, Wechsler argued. He noted that the Court had judged other areas—contempt, disorderly conduct, obscenity, and sedition—"in terms that satisfy the First Amendment."

Freedom of speech was a "national commitment," he said, that had been upheld repeatedly by the Court.

Quoting from a number of past decisions and historic documents, Wechsler stressed the importance of freedom of speech and the press in a democracy. In particular, the Court had protected the right to criticize public officials and government action. Such freedom, he noted, quoting from the *Roth* case, "was fashioned to assure unfettered interchange of ideas for the bringing about of political and social changes desired by the people." The Court recognized, Wechsler said, that such discussion could sometimes be raucous, rude, and contentious. Here, Wechsler quoted Justice Hugo L. Black, whose majority opinion in the 1941 case *Bridges* v. *California* allowed citizens to criticize judges:

> For it is a prized American privilege to speak one's
> mind, although not always with perfect good taste,
> on all public institutions.

Just as speech that was not necessarily in good taste fell under the protection of the First Amendment, so too, did speech that was not necessarily true, or able to be proved true in a court of law, Wechsler wrote. He cited the Court's decision in *Cantwell* v. *Connecticut*, a case involving two members of the Jehovah's Witnesses who were convicted for breach of the peace after broadcasting anti-Catholic messages. In a unanimous decision the Supreme Court overturned the conviction and held that laws to maintain order could not be used to suppress the "free communication of views." Wechsler quoted Justice Owen Roberts's decision in the case:

> In the realm of religious faith, and in that of polit-
> ical belief, sharp differences arise. In both fields
> the tenets of one man may seem the rankest error
> to his neighbor. To persuade others to his own

point of view, the pleader, as we know, at times, resorts to exaggeration, to vilification of men who have been, or are, prominent in church or state, and even to false statement. But the people of this nation have ordained in the light of history, that, in spite of the probability of excesses and abuses, these liberties are, in the long view, essential to enlightened opinion and right conduct on the part of the citizens of a democracy.

The First Amendment also protected speech even if it maligned public officials, Wechsler contended. "If political criticism could be punished on the ground that it endangers the esteem with which its object is regarded," he noted, "none safely could be uttered that was anything but praise."

In the next pages, Wechsler discussed the Sedition Act of 1798, comparing it to the libel law in the *Sullivan* case. The act made it a crime to "write, print, utter or publish . . . any false, scandalous and malicious writing or writings against the government of the United States, or either house of the Congress . . . , or the President." As in the Alabama libel law, those charged under the act could defend themselves by proving what they said was true. But often, as Congressman John Nicholas of Virginia argued during debate on the act, such proof was hard to get. Nicholas argued that the act would not only stop newspapers from printing falsehoods but would also prevent them from reporting the truth.

Wechsler used Nicholas's words to drive home his point. Newspapers "would be deterred from printing anything which should be in the least offensive to a power which might so greatly harass them. They would not only refrain from publishing anything of the least questionable nature, but they would be afraid of publishing the truth, as, though true, it might not always be in their power to establish the truth to the satisfaction of a court of justice."

Even though the Supreme Court had never ruled on the Sedition Act, Wechsler argued that the fact that it had been discredited should carry at least as much weight as past Court rulings. "Though the Sedition Act was never passed on by this Court, the verdict of history surely sustains the view that it was inconsistent with the First Amendment," the *Times*'s lawyer wrote. The Alabama libel law, he contended, was even more repressive than the Sedition Act. Because it was civil and not criminal law, the defendant did not have to be proved guilty beyond a reasonable doubt. The law imposed no limit on the amount of damages (or how many times the defendant could be sued for the same offense), while the act had a set fine.

Wechsler argued that the Fourteenth Amendment required that states, like the federal government, had to abide by the First Amendment. He dismissed the Alabama Supreme Court's assertion that the Fourteenth Amendment did not apply to the case because it dealt only with state action and not private action. Clearly, Wechsler argued, the state had involved itself in the *Sullivan* case. Sullivan had used a state law to take the *Times* to court, and a state court had issued the judgment in the case.

In ruling against the *Times*, the brief continued, the lower court had never tried to balance the two interests in the case: freedom of the press versus an official's reputation. It had merely ruled in favor of the official without considering press freedom at all. The Court "must weigh the impact of the [critical] words against the protection given by the principles of the First Amendment," the brief contended. The quotation came from *Pennekamp* v. *Florida*, a Supreme Court decision that had allowed criticism of a judge even if it contained "half-truths."

Wechsler contended that the court could have ordered

other ways to protect both press freedom and reputation. Some other courts, he noted, required a person filing a suit to prove that the words were printed with malice, with the intention of harming an official's reputation.

Anyone accusing a public official of libel had to meet the standard of proving actual malice, the brief noted. States protected officials from libel in that way to ensure that damage suits did not "inhibit the fearless, vigorous, and effective administration of policies of government." Ordinary citizens and the press, Wechsler argued, should have the same protection.

Wechsler debunked the claim that a commercial advertisement did not qualify for press freedom. The ad, he wrote, represented "the daily dialogue of politics" and should be considered "political criticism" or "political expression." As such, it should be protected by the First Amendment. He also disputed Sullivan's assertion that the ad libeled him. Wechsler pointed out that the ad had never mentioned the commissioner by name and that Sullivan had never shown that it had damaged his reputation. Moreover, the false portions of the ad that referred to the police (Martin Luther King Jr. was arrested four times, not seven; and the police did not "ring" the campus but patrolled it in large numbers) were only discrepancies, not injurious enough to be considered libel.

Next, Wechsler objected to the "shockingly excessive" amount of damages imposed by the court. Because newspapers would hesitate to publish anything controversial if faced with huge financial penalties, the *Sullivan* award interfered with freedom of the press, according to the brief. Suspending reports on the South during the midst of the civil rights battle—certainly a major controversy—would make a mockery of press freedom and harm the nation. "[I]f a judgment of this size can be sustained upon such facts as these, its repressive influence will extend far beyond deterring such inaccuracies of assertion as have been established here," Wechsler wrote. "This is not a time—there never is a time—when it would serve the values enshrined in the Constitution to force the press to curtail its attention to the tensest issues that confront the country or to forego the dissemination of its publications in the areas where tension is extreme."

Wechsler devoted the final pages of the brief to his contention that the *Times* was not an Alabama business and that the suit should have been tried in federal, not state, court.

Ministers Make Their Case
The black ministers, in their brief for the accompanying case, argued that they had not known about the ad before it was published and had never given consent for their names to be used in it. The libel verdict, they said, violated their constitutional rights to due process and equality under the law. The brief also contended that the "atmosphere of racial bias, passion and hostile community pressures," the bias of the judge, and the rejection of black jurors all played a role in the verdict.

Two Briefs for Sullivan
Roland Nachman Jr. represented Sullivan before the Supreme Court, as he had in the lower courts. Nachman, a Montgomery attorney, had as regular clients the *Montgomery Advertiser* and the *Alabama Journal*. The newspapers agreed to let him take Sullivan's case, apparently not seeing his participation as a conflict of interest. Nachman later served as vice president of the Alabama Bar Association.

In his sixty-nine-page brief, Nachman noted that the accounts in the ad about police activities were untrue and defamed Sullivan. Nachman rejected Wechsler's constitutional claims. "[L]ibelous utterances have never been protected by the Federal Constitution," he noted. He quoted the Court's decisions in both *Beauharnais* and *Roth* that "certain forms of speech"—in this case libel—were "considered outside the scope of constitutional protection." In addition, Nachman wrote, commercial advertising did not qualify for the First Amendment protections afforded speech and the press.

To bolster his point, Sullivan's lawyer used the same quote from Thomas Jefferson that had supported the Court's decision in the *Beauharnais* case. The great free-speech advocate, in a letter to Abigail Adams, wrote that even though the Sedition Act of 1798, which he opposed, was no longer in force, individual states had the power to restrain "the overwhelming torrent of slander which is confounding all vice and virtue, all truth and falsehood in the U.S." Jefferson added: "While we deny that Congress have a right to control the freedom of the press, we have ever asserted the right of the states, and their exclusive right, to do so."

Nachman made much of the fact that the Court had consistently upheld the right of states to deal with libel— and with good reason. If the Court barred the states from enforcing libel laws, he argued, it would result in "the confiscation of the rights of those defamed." Critics would be able to accuse public officials of egregious, and false, actions. Granted immunity from libel, these critics could charge (falsely) that "the Secretary of State had given military secrets to the enemy; that the Secretary of the Treasury had embezzled public funds; that the Governor of a state poisoned his wife," according to Nachman.

He cited an opinion written by Judge William Howard Taft (who later became president and then chief justice of the U.S. Supreme Court) in a similar case involving the *Cincinnati Post* and a political candidate named Theodore F. Hallam, who claimed the newspaper had defamed him.

In writing the decision for the U.S. Court of Appeals for the Sixth Circuit, Judge Taft upheld a $2,500 judgment against the *Post*. A newspaper that printed falsehoods, even if they were printed in good faith, should be subject to libel laws, the judge ruled. Otherwise, the nation would suffer because good candidates would not want to risk their reputation by running for office. Taft wrote:

> If the privilege is to extend to cases like that at bar, then a man who offers himself as a candidate must submit uncomplainingly to the loss of his reputation . . . whenever an untrue charge of disgraceful conduct is made against him, if only his accuser honestly believes the charge upon reasonable ground. We think that not only is such a sacrifice not required of everyone who consents to become a candidate for office, but that to sanction such a doctrine would do the public more harm than good.

Addressing another of Wechsler's points, Nachman defended the lower court's holding that the ad was libelous *per se*. The ad, he wrote, was unquestionably libelous. "This publication charged a public official in devastating fashion with departing from all civilized standards of law and decency in the administration of his official duties," Nachman noted.

He also defended the large damage award. Citing *Beauharnais* and lower court decisions, he maintained that the fine served to deter the defendant from libeling again. Such fines, he asserted in a footnote, served to warn others against such behavior and were "punishment for gross misbehavior for the good of the public." He noted that New York state and federal courts had recently awarded even higher damages to plaintiffs in libel suits.

COMMISSIONER SULLIVAN'S LAWYER CITED AN OPINION BY JUDGE WILLIAM
HOWARD TAFT TO BOLSTER HIS CLIENT'S CASE.

Nachman relied on the Seventh Amendment to but-
tress his next argument: It was up to the jury, not the judge
or the Court, to set damages. The Supreme Court, he
argued, should not interfere with the jury's interpretation
of the facts of the case. The Seventh Amendment established the right of citizens to have a trial by jury and further

stipulated that "no fact tried by a jury, shall be otherwise re-examined in any Court of the United States, than according to the rules of the common law."

Finally, Nachman attacked the *Times*'s contention that it was not an Alabama business and therefore the case should not have been tried in state courts. "If financial reward comes to the *Times* from its on-the-spot news coverage in Alabama, it is fair that citizens of Alabama should be able to sue the *Times* here when it has wronged them," Sullivan's lawyer wrote.

In his brief addressing the black ministers' claims, Nachman dismissed the complaints about the conduct of the trial. He maintained that by remaining silent and by their later actions, the ministers showed they approved of the ad. Concluding the short brief, Nachman said his client "care[d] deeply" about freedom of speech and of the press. "And he is also concerned," the brief added, "that these basic freedoms do not degenerate into a license to lie."

During this time, several other libel suits had been filed against the media, including a second suit against the *Times* for news reports on the civil rights campaign and one against CBS for a program the network aired on attempts to prevent blacks in Montgomery from voting. The *Chicago Tribune*, in its brief, predicted that "national reporting and editorial commentary" in the nation's media would be "dealt a severe setback" if the *Sullivan* judgment was allowed to stand. "No newspaper, regardless of its size, can afford the risk of lawsuits across the country in whatever locales the complainants may select," the brief said.

In its brief, the *Washington Post* claimed that the libel suit against the *Times* was part of a widespread effort to prevent the media from reporting the violent clashes taking place in the South over racial integration and the push for black equality. The *Sullivan* suit, according to the *Post*'s brief, was "part of a broad attempt by officials in Alabama to invoke the libel laws against all those who had the temerity to criticize Alabama's conduct in the intense racial conflict." When the *Sullivan* case finally came before the Supreme Court in 1964, media outlets faced almost $300 million in libel suits filed by public officials in the South.

The ACLU brief defended the right of organizations to publish political or editorial ads to raise money and call attention to their cause. If the Court did not overturn the *Sullivan* ruling, the brief said, the freedom of dissenting groups to express their views would be "greatly diminished."

The briefs were filed with the Supreme Court in the fall of 1963. These lengthy documents provided the justices with the facts of the cases and a discussion of the issues involved. Before they voted on the cases, however, the justices would question the lawyers on both sides during oral arguments.

SIX
ORAL ARGUMENTS

COURT OBSERVERS HAVE OFTEN SAID that a lawyer rarely wins a case during oral arguments, but that he or she can lose a case with a poor presentation. Even the most experienced lawyers have admitted to sleepless nights before appearing in front of the nation's highest court. The walk up the majestic marble stairs is long indeed. Sitting in the austere courtroom, surrounded by marble and mahogany, lawyers anxiously await the arrival of the black-robed justices. White quill pens placed at the counsel tables remind the participants of the long list of historic cases that have been decided in this room.

Before stepping out from behind the red velvet curtains, each justice shakes hands with all the others. The practice began with Chief Justice Melville W. Fuller in the 1890s. Fuller used the handshakes to remind justices that differences of opinion in the courtroom should not deter them from their united dedication to justice and the rule of law.

WECHSLER ARGUES HIS CASE
At 12:30 P.M. on Monday, January 6, 1964, Chief Justice Earl Warren opened the afternoon session of the U.S. Supreme Court. Chief Justice Warren, appointed in 1953 by President Dwight D. Eisenhower, had led the Court on a new course, beginning with the landmark decision in

CHIEF JUSTICE EARL WARREN, LEFT, REACHES FOR A PAMPHLET HANDED TO HIM BY A PICKETER DEMANDING HIS IMPEACHMENT.

Brown v. *Board of Education* that American public schools could no longer be segregated. Since that controversial decision, the Court had ruled on a string of cases that defended the individual rights of Americans, including protection against unreasonable search and seizure, the right to an attorney, and equal rights at the ballot box.

Chief Justice Warren sat in the center of the raised bench in the front of the courtroom. The most senior justice, Hugo L. Black, sat at Warren's right, with William O. Douglas, the next longest-serving justice, at his left. The remaining justices alternated between right and left, in order of their years of service: Tom C. Clark, John M.

Harlan, William J. Brennan Jr., Potter Stewart, Byron R. White, and Arthur J. Goldberg.

Chief Justice Warren asked Herbert Wechsler to present the *New York Times*'s case. The lawyer began with his claim that the *Sullivan* decision threatened freedom of the press "with a dimension not confronted since the early days of the Republic." How far can state officials go, he asked, in using libel charges to punish newspapers that have published articles critical of the officials? And, he asked, how far beyond state borders can officials reach to get at a newspaper located a thousand miles away?

After answering the justices' questions about the other pending libel suits, Wechsler described the ad, quoting passages and explaining its purpose. The text, he told the justices, was "a statement of protest . . . interwoven, to be sure, with a recitation of events." He noted that the ad "names no names" and "plainly makes no personal attack on any individual."

The prestige of those endorsing the ad, Wechsler said, led the *Times* to accept it for publication without question. At this point, the lawyer read the parts of the ad that Sullivan believed libeled him. These paragraphs, Wechsler acknowledged, contained errors, which he pointed out to the justices. He also noted that the paragraph that referred to "Southern violators" never once mentioned the city of Montgomery. He agreed with Justice Goldberg that the events described in the ad could have occurred anywhere in the South.

Under questioning from Justice Brennan, Wechsler said he was "at a loss to know precisely" how the ad libeled Sullivan. But he noted that Sullivan had claimed that the references to Montgomery and police action reflected on him as police commissioner.

Justice White asked if the ad could refer to the state police rather than the local police. Wechsler said it could have. On the other hand, the lawyer said, the charge that the dining hall was padlocked definitely referred to state authorities. "That grievance has just absolutely nothing to do with the respondent," Wechsler said.

All told, the errors in the ad amounted to "very small discrepancies indeed between what was said and what the record shows to have been the case," he told the Court. Sullivan's claim that almost the entire ad referred to him because the police were mentioned in a few cases was "fantastic," according to Wechsler. Nevertheless, he said, the circuit court judge accepted Sullivan's view and allowed him to disprove charges that had never been made. "[T]he trial court permitted him solemnly to prove that he hadn't really bombed Dr. King's home, and that the police in fact had done everything they could to solve that atrocious crime, had worked overtime on it and so on, which of course was not challenged by anybody."

Wechsler said the *Times* had printed a retraction that reported the ad's errors. The retraction came at Governor Patterson's request and said that the newspaper had not intended to imply that the governor was guilty of misconduct. Wechsler said this was printed "in deference to the high office" of the governor.

Sullivan's request for a similar retraction, however, was met with puzzlement, the lawyer said. "[T]hey couldn't see how [the third paragraph] or anything else referred to Commissioner Sullivan," Wechsler told the justices.

The lawyer zeroed in on his major defense—that the First Amendment protected the paper's right to publish the ad. The lower courts, he said, denied that defense, saying only "that the First Amendment did not protect libelous statements." The jury, however, never got a chance to judge whether the statements were libelous because Judge Walter Jones had ruled that they were libelous *per se.*

SUPREME COURT JUSTICE ARTHUR J. GOLDBERG, APPOINTED TO THE COURT BY PRESIDENT JOHN F. KENNEDY IN 1962, WAS ONE OF NINE JUSTICES TO HEAR THE *SULLIVAN* CASE.

In response to a question from Justice Goldberg, Wechsler noted that any criticism of a government department would be presumed to be directed at the head of the department.

"I can't say that the New York police tap wires, for example," Wechsler said, "though I believe they do, without giving Commissioner Murphy an axe against me, since it's illegal for them to do it without a court order in New York under the federal law."

In Alabama, the lawyer continued, a public official could be awarded unlimited damages for published state-ments that criticized his department's actions. As long as the court agreed that the statements were harmful and the jury decided that they referred to the public official, damages could be set at any amount. Under this system of law, Wechsler said, the only defense would be to prove that each part of the statement was true.

The legal system allowed states to set their own libel and slander laws. But, Wechsler said, when Alabama applied its libel law to criticism of public officials, the state violated the First Amendment. "The First Amendment," Wechsler told the Court, "was precisely designed to do away with seditious libel, . . . the punishment of criticism of the Government and criticism of officials." That protection applied to everyone, not just to newspapers, he said.

Wechsler noted that the Court had never ruled on the Sedition Act of 1798 (it expired before a case came before the Court). But he argued that the Court had made rulings granting First Amendment protections in cases involving obscenity and contempt. Like libel, those areas had never been under the protection of the First Amendment before the Court rulings. The *Sullivan* case, he noted, presented the Court for the first time with an opportunity to rule on the constitutionality of libel laws.

The First Amendment's author, James Madison himself, would have supported his argument, Wechsler contended. During the time the Bill of Rights was written, he said, critics often made unsubstantiated charges against their opponents in the press. "In the historic period in which Madison was writing," he told the Court, "charges of bribery were common, and it was this type of press freedom that he saw in the First Amendment."

But under Alabama libel law, according to Wechsler, a person (or entity) could be found guilty of libel even when only commenting on someone or something unless all the facts of the case were correct.

Wechsler proposed that public officials should never

JAMES MADISON, THE AUTHOR OF THE FIRST AMENDMENT, BELIEVED STRONGLY IN THE FREEDOM OF THE PRESS.

be able to sue for libel, even if a citizen maliciously—and falsely—accused him of wrongdoing. Instead, he suggested, the official could make a speech answering his critics. "And that, of course, is what most mayors do," he said, "and what the political history of the country has produced."

The lawyer acknowledged that the Court might want to consider ways to protect officials from vicious, false attacks. But such protections should never outweigh freedom of discussion. Other remedies, Wechsler said, included printing a notice in the paper or other media.

Some states allowed damages only for actual monetary losses that could be proved to be the result of the libel. And in cases like *Sullivan*, he said, the Court might have to review the evidence to make certain the verdict did not infringe on free speech. (Usually appeals courts, including the U.S. Supreme Court, consider only the issues involved in a case and leave the lower courts to rule on the facts of the case.)

Allowing juries to make unlimited awards of damages in libel cases, Wechsler said, presented a real threat to press freedom. Such large damage awards amounted to "a death penalty for any newspaper if multiplied," he told the justices.

Wechsler spent the next several minutes making his case that the ad did not, in fact, specifically refer to the police commissioner. "The record shows there were 175 policemen, that there was a police chief in addition to the Commissioner, and there is not the slightest bit of sug- gestion here, . . . that what the police did they were ordered to do by Commissioner Sullivan as the City Commissioner with jurisdiction over the police," Wechsler said in answer to a question posed by Justice Black.

NacHman Takes HIs Turn BeFore THe court

After the *Times*'s lawyer answered a few more questions, a red light on the lectern started to blink, indicating that his time was up. He sat down, and M. Roland Nachman stood up to begin his defense of Sullivan. Nachman told the jus- tices that he sharply disagreed with Wechsler over the facts of the case. "We say there was ample and, indeed, overwhelming evidence to support the jury verdict." He noted that the *Times* had never contended that the ad was true in its pleadings. Quoting testimony from the trial,

Nachman argued that the *Times* had admitted from the beginning of the case that the ad was "completely false."

At this point, Justice Goldberg questioned Nachman's claim. "I looked over the record, and I thought there was evidence at the trial which showed the truth in part of some of the allegations of the ad," he told Nachman. Sullivan's lawyer later clarified that he was referring only to two paragraphs (three and six). But he clung to his claim that those sections were entirely false.

The statements of witnesses and the *Times*'s own admissions were part of the evidence that went to the jurors and led to their verdict, according to Nachman. It was not the role of the U.S. Supreme Court, the attorney said, to second-guess the jury and reexamine the facts. He further argued that libel cases fell under state control. Libel was not protected by the First Amendment and, he told the justices, the Court had no business ruling on cases which clearly dealt with libelous statements, as the *Sullivan* case did.

"Up to now, as we read the cases, the Court has left the characterization of publications as libelous or not libelous to the states," Nachman pointed out. The Court could rightly rule on cases where innocuous words had been falsely labeled as libelous, Nachman said. "If a statement was made that somebody had blond hair and a state court held that this statement was libelous *per se*, well, of course this Court could review it." But the *Sullivan* case dealt with statements that were clearly libelous, Nachman said. "It charges [the police] with criminal offenses, charges which would certainly hold them up to contempt and ridicule and disapproval, and we think we're well within the classic definition of libel."

Under questioning from Justice Goldberg, Nachman quoted the passages in the ad he believed referred to his client. He listed the police actions described in paragraph three, including the padlocking of the dining hall. He also contended that it could reasonably be assumed that the word "they" in paragraph six could apply to police and to commissioner Sullivan. That would tie the commissioner to the bombing and the assault of Dr. King, as well as to the arrests for loitering and speeding, according to Nachman.

Justice Goldberg noted that "they" and "Southern violators" could refer to any resident of the South. What would prevent a law-abiding Southern citizen from filing a similar suit? Goldberg asked.

Nachman replied that state law did not allow libel suits by large groups. A person could file for libel only when he or she could be easily identified as the member of the group targeted by libelous statements. In the *Sullivan* case, he noted, people naturally thought of the police commissioner as the person responsible for police actions.

Sullivan was entitled to special damages, Nachman said, because the ad's claims might make it hard for him to get a job in the future. Sullivan did not prove that he had suffered any actual damages, Nachman acknowledged. But the lawyer recounted the testimony of Sullivan's former employer that he would not rehire Sullivan if he believed the ad's charges. In addition, Nachman noted, Sullivan was entitled to punitive damages, assessed to prevent the *Times* from repeating its actions.

The Alabama libel law did not abridge First Amendment rights, he asserted, because the press could have avoided hefty fines by retracting the statements made about the police or by proving the truth of the ad. What the *Times* asked for—"absolute immunity against a libel suit" involving public officials—was "something brand new" in U.S. law, Nachman told the justices. "We think it would have a devastating effect on this nation."

Justice White modified that position slightly, asking if newspapers could be granted immunity if they believed they were publishing the truth about officials. Nachman strenuously objected:

> We submit that this Court and no other court has ever made a distinction between libel of public officials and libel of private persons. Public officials . . . have a right to sue for libel when they have been defamed.

With his time nearly up, Nachman argued that the damages awarded Sullivan were not excessive. A smaller amount, he told the Court, "would have been a slap on the wrist to the *Times* for this sort of conduct." As the light blinked on, Nachman concluded his argument and returned to his seat. The Court adjourned.

Arguments Presented in Ministers' Case

The following day, the lawyers addressed the case against the black ministers. Samuel R. Pierce Jr., who had served as a New York judge, and former U.S. Attorney General William P. Rogers spoke on behalf of the ministers. Rogers had also helped write the *amicus* brief filed by the *Washington Post* in the earlier *Sullivan* case.

Taking his turn before the bench, Rogers told the justices that the *Sullivan* ruling was the "most serious threat to freedom of the press in this century." He noted that newspapers had no way of checking the accuracy of everything they printed.

Pierce told the Court that the suit had been filed to "suppress and punish the voices for racial equality." The lawyer also detailed the racist attitudes and behaviors in evidence at the trial. The ministers' black lawyers, he noted, had not even been addressed as "Mr." during the trial.

During his arguments, Nachman once again defended

the Alabama libel law and the court rulings. He told the justices that the ministers' failure to answer Sullivan's letter demanding a retraction proved they had gone along with the ad. Chief Justice Warren took exception to that, however. After the *Brown* v. *Board of Education* ruling that had ordered school desegregation, Warren had received much hate mail, including charges that he had libeled various people. "If he [Warren] has made no such statements, must he reply or suffer a one-half million dollar libel judgment?" Warren asked Nachman. Sullivan's attorney did not back down. He defended the Alabama law that silence indicated approval.

seven
A DECISION WORTHY OF "DANCING IN THE STREETS"

WITH THE ORAL ARGUMENTS in both cases at an end, the lawyers and their clients could only wait for a decision. The justices' work, however, had only started. Meeting in a private conference room at the Court, they spent long hours discussing the case and the thorny issues involved.

After debating issues and reviewing a case thoroughly, the justices take an initial vote. If the chief justice votes with the majority, he writes the decision for the Court or appoints an associate justice also on the winning side to take on the task. When the chief justice is on the losing side, the most-senior associate justice who has voted with the majority makes the assignment. Justices on either side often write separate opinions expressing their views on the case. Sometimes, after reading the drafts, justices change their vote. If the vote shifts to the other side, then a new decision must be written by a justice voting with the majority.

SWEEPING NEW PRESS PROTECTIONS

In the *Sullivan* case, Chief Justice Earl Warren assigned Justice William J. Brennan Jr. to write the majority opinion. In his efforts to win unanimous support for the decision, Justice Brennan wrote eight drafts before all the justices finally agreed and gave their approval.

JUSTICE WILLIAM J. BRENNAN JR. WROTE EIGHT DRAFTS OF THE *SULLIVAN*
OPINION BEFORE WINNING THE SUPPORT OF ALL OF HIS COLLEAGUES.

On March 9, 1964, two months and two days after the
final arguments in the *Sullivan* case, the U.S. Supreme
Court issued its unanimous decision. The opinion overturned the rulings in both *Sullivan* cases. For the first
time, the Court recognized the threat to free speech and a
free press posed by libel suits, and set limits on the damages a state could award public officials who sued for libel.

The landmark decision gave sweeping new protections to the press and free speech. The ruling protected

even speech that was false. Under its provisions, public officials could collect for libel only if they could prove that false statements were made with "actual malice"—that the speaker or the press used the words knowing that the statements were false or with "reckless disregard" to whether the statements were true or false. Throughout the decision, Justice Brennan borrowed phrases from and cited many of the cases *Times* attorney Herbert Wechsler had used in his brief.

Two justices—Arthur J. Goldberg and Hugo L. Black—issued separate concurring opinions that called for even stronger free-speech protections. They would eliminate all curbs on criticism of public officials, even false and malicious statements. In their view, public officials should not be allowed to sue for libel, even when statements were false and malicious. Justice William O. Douglas joined both concurrences.

In his decision, Justice Brennan said that Alabama's libel law did not safeguard freedom of the press and of speech as required by the First and Fourteenth Amendments. Brennan quickly dismissed the Alabama Supreme Court's contention that the Fourteenth Amendment did not apply in the case. Civil cases fell under the amendment's protection, Brennan said, when the state used its power to try cases and administer judgments.

Just as quickly, the justice dispensed with the argument that the ad was "commercial speech" and therefore did not qualify for free-speech protections. Brennan noted that the ad "communicated information, expressed opinion, recited grievances, protested claimed abuses, and sought financial support on behalf of a movement whose existence and objectives are matters of the highest public interest and concern." People depended on these types of ads to get their message out, Brennan said. If these "editorial" ads were not protected, it would "shackle the First Amendment in its attempt to secure 'the widest possible dissemination of information from diverse and antagonistic sources.'"

Brennan then tackled the central issue in the case: whether the state's libel law abridged freedom of speech and of the press. Echoing Wechsler, the justice said that past Supreme Court decisions showed "a profound national commitment to the principle that debate on public issues should be uninhibited, robust, and wide-open, and that it may well include vehement, caustic, and sometimes unpleasantly sharp attacks on government and public officials."

By those standards, Brennan asserted, the ad in the *Times* "would seem clearly to qualify for the constitutional protections." That the ad contained errors, Brennan stated, did not exempt it from the First Amendment's protection. "[The] erroneous statement is inevitable in free debate and . . . it must be protected if the freedoms of expression are to have the 'breathing space' that they 'need . . . to survive.'"

Nor could the First Amendment's protections be nullified because a speech damaged an official's reputation, Brennan said. He cited two cases highlighted in Wechsler's brief, the *Bridges* decision that allowed criticism of judges and the *Pennekamp* case, which protected such criticism even when it contained "half-truths" and "misinformation." Public officials, like judges, should be treated as "men of fortitude, able to thrive in a hardy climate," Brennan said. "Criticism of their official conduct does not lose its constitutional protection merely because it is effective criticism and hence diminishes their official reputations."

Following Wechsler's lead, Brennan condemned the Sedition Act of 1798. "Although the Sedition Act was never tested in this Court, the attack upon its validity has carried the day in the court of history," he said. The act, he noted, had been discredited because "the restraint it imposed upon criticism of government and public officials . . . was inconsistent with the First Amendment." In essence, Brennan's opinion declared the Sedition Act unconstitutional.

The justice reiterated James Madison's concept of government: "The people, not the government, possess the absolute sovereignty."

State as well as federal laws, Justice Brennan noted, had to comply with the First Amendment. The Fourteenth Amendment made that a requirement, according to several past Court rulings. And states could not use civil law to avoid First Amendment protections required of criminal law, Brennan said. Fear of the penalties allowed by Alabama's civil libel law, he noted, could be "markedly more inhibiting" than the fear of prosecution on criminal libel charges. "The judgment awarded in this case—without the need for any proof of actual pecuniary loss—was one thousand times greater than the maximum fine provided by the Alabama criminal statute, and one hundred times greater than that provided by the Sedition Act," Brennan said. He added that newspapers could face an unlimited number of lawsuits over one statement. Even if a newspaper could pay off all the damages awarded, the suits would create an atmosphere "of fear and timidity" that would deter news media from criticizing public officials and repress free speech and press freedom.

First Amendment rights also covered statements that were not true, Brennan ruled. If critics had to prove the truth of everything they said, then they would censor themselves. This would block not only false speech but also true statements that might be difficult to prove.

Under libel law like that in Alabama, Brennan noted, those who would otherwise criticize public officials' conduct might keep quiet even though they believed their criticism was true and even though it was in fact true because they were not sure they could prove it in court and they did not want to face the expense of a lawsuit. The law "thus dampens the vigor and limits the variety of public debate," Brennan found. "It is inconsistent with the First and Fourteenth Amendments."

The Court's ruling struck down Alabama's libel law as it applied to public officials. State libel laws would have to meet First Amendment requirements. From then on, public officials would be able to collect damages for harm to their reputation only if they proved in court that the hurtful statements were made with actual malice. Brennan defined "actual malice" as "knowledge that [the statement] was false or with reckless disregard of whether it was false or not."

This shifted the burden of proof from the defendant in a libel case to the public official suing for libel. It also gave citizens and the press the same protections public officials had.

The decision overturned the judge's ruling that the *Times* ad was libelous *per se*. Libel could no longer be presumed malicious, Brennan said; malice had to be proved.

When the Supreme Court reverses a judgment, the case often returns to the lower court for a new hearing or trial. Any new judgment must follow the rules established by the Supreme Court's decision.

In the case of *Sullivan*, however, the Court knew that another Montgomery jury might well decide that Sullivan had proved malice and grant a second large damage award. The Court wanted to prevent the official in this case and those in future cases from using libel law to put financial pressure on their critics. Nothing in the Constitution gave the Court the power to determine the amount of damages in the case. But in his decision, Justice Brennan overruled the jury's interpretation of the evidence. The Court was justified in examining the evidence—the jury's job—to ensure "effective judicial administration," Brennan said. "This Court's duty is not limited to the elaboration of constitutional principles; we must also in proper cases review the evidence to make certain that those principles have been constitutionally applied."

The evidence showed that Sullivan had failed to prove that the *Times* or the ministers had acted with actual malice, Brennan said. Sullivan did not demonstrate "the convincing clarity which the constitutional standard demands." He said the *Times* may have been negligent in not checking the ad's facts, but the paper's actions were not reckless enough to be considered malicious.

In addition, Brennan wrote, the evidence failed to prove that the ad targeted Sullivan personally. The state supreme court's ruling that allowed damages to a public official for criticism aimed at general government misdeeds had "disquieting implications for criticism of government conduct," Brennan said. Such a ruling could effectively silence all government critics, since the criticism could always be indirectly tied to the officials in charge. That interpretation of the law, Brennan concluded, "strikes at the very center of the constitutionally protected area of free expression."

With that, he ended his opinion and reversed the judgments against the *Times* and the four ministers.

TWO CONCURRING OPINIONS

The two concurring opinions both argued that people and the press should be free to criticize government and its officials without any restrictions at all. Justice Black, in his opinion, argued that the First Amendment completely banned states from requiring those who criticized the conduct of public officials to pay damages for their comments. Black noted that malice was difficult to define, "an elusive, abstract concept, hard to prove and hard to disprove." Requiring officials to prove malice did not protect speech sufficiently and merely served as a "stopgap measure," the justice said.

It did not matter whether the ad aimed its statements at Sullivan, the damage award was excessive, or the ministers signed the ad, Black said. He voted to overturn the lower court rulings "exclusively on the ground that the *Times* and the individual defendants had an absolute, unconditional constitutional right to publish in the *Times* advertisement their criticisms of the Montgomery agencies and officials."

The high damage awards in the *Sullivan* case, however, provided "dramatic proof" that "state libel laws threaten the very existence of an American press virile enough to publish unpopular views on public affairs and bold enough to criticize the conduct of public officials," according to the justice. He noted that the *Sullivan* case probably had as much to do with Montgomery's opposition to desegregation as to the damages alleged by the commissioner. And he warned of other "huge verdicts lurking just around the corner." In Alabama alone, eleven libel suits seeking $5.6 million from the *Times* and $1.7 million from the Columbia Broadcasting System had been filed, Black noted. He predicted that proponents of other causes would adopt "this technique for harassing and punishing a free press," to stop criticism of their behavior.

The First Amendment, Black continued, "no more permits the States to impose damages for libel than it does the Federal Government."

Americans must have the freedom to discuss the conduct of the public officials elected to serve them, Black

JUSTICE HUGO L. BLACK VOTED WITH THE MAJORITY IN THE *SULLIVAN* CASE,
BUT HE BELIEVED THE FIRST AMENDMENT GRANTED THE PRESS MUCH
BROADER FREEDOMS THAN JUSTICE BRENNAN'S DECISION ALLOWED.

said. Using libel awards to penalize those who criticize
the government and its officials "shut off discussion of the
very kind most needed." He concluded the short opinion
with a warning: "This Nation, I suspect, can live in peace
without libel suits based on public discussions of public
affairs and public officials. But I doubt that a country can
live in freedom where its people can be made to suffer
physically or financially for criticizing their government,
its actions, or its officials."

Like Black, Justice Goldberg argued for "an absolute, unconditional privilege [for citizens and the press] to criticize official conduct despite the harm which may flow from excesses and abuses." The right to speak one's mind about the government should not be jeopardized by a jury's decision on the speaker's motivation, the justice said. He noted that those who seek public office must expect criticism of their actions. Since previous Court rulings banned the government from filing libel suits, Goldberg argued, similar suits filed by public officials should also be banned.

He acknowledged that some might argue that "deliberately and maliciously false statements" had "no conceivable value as free speech." But, Goldberg pointed out, as Brennan and Black had, that libel laws target more than malicious speech; they threaten all free speech. "If individual citizens may be held liable in damages for strong words, which a jury finds false and maliciously motivated, there can be little doubt that public debate and advocacy will be constrained." The opinion of the Court, he noted, "conclusively demonstrates the chilling effect of the Alabama libel laws on First Amendment freedoms in the area of race relations."

Justice Goldberg made it clear that he supported a ban on libel only when statements involved officials' public duties. They should be able to sue for malicious statements made about their private lives, the justice said. "Purely private defamation has little to do with the political ends of a self-governing society," Goldberg noted.

A good argument—not libel suits—would serve to protect public officials who believed they had been unfairly criticized, the justice said. He concluded with a quote from Justice Louis D. Brandeis: "Sunlight is the most powerful of all disinfectants."

JUSTICES SPEAK THEIR MINDS: HOW SEPARATE OPINIONS INFLUENCE LAW

The U.S. Supreme Court is the highest court in the land. Its decisions are final. A Supreme Court decision can be overturned only by another decision issued by a later Court or by a constitutional amendment. Among the most notable decisions later invalidated was the *Dred Scott* ruling, in which the Court determined that blacks were not citizens and were not entitled to protection by the federal government. The decision was overturned by the Thirteenth and Fourteenth Amendments, which abolished slavery and established that everyone born in the United States was automatically a citizen with equal rights.

Usually the Court bases its decisions on precedent, rulings that previous Courts have made. Only in extreme circumstances does the Court reverse an earlier decision.

The majority opinion—the ruling agreed to by five or more justices—establishes the law in the matter. A ruling requires only a simple majority—five of the nine justices on a full Court. The justices, appointed for life, each have an equal vote. Usually the chief justice, if he agrees with the majority, either writes the majority decision himself or appoints an associate justice also on the winning side to take on the task. When the chief justice is on the losing side, the most-senior associate justice who has voted with the majority makes the assignment.

Justices can write their own opinions on any case they wish. If they agree with the majority vote but have different reasons for their views, or want to comment on the case further, they can submit a concurrence. Those who disagree with a majority opinion can submit a dissent. Sometimes a justice writes a separate opinion so well that other justices are persuaded to join the dissent or concurrence. Occasionally enough justices decide to join a separate opinion that it becomes the majority opinion. At times, the vote has shifted sides when justices withdrew from the majority decision to join a dissent.

Justice Tom Clark once said, "You know, we don't have money at the Court for an army, and we can't take ads in the newspapers, and we don't want to go out on a picket line in our robes. We have to convince the nation by the force of our opinions." That force can be—and occasionally is—undermined by opposing justices' separate opinions in a case. If a case is particularly controversial, a justice's separate opinion—sometimes concurring, but more often dissenting—can encourage continued opposition to the ruling. That is the reason Chief Justice Earl Warren worked so hard to get a unanimous ruling in *Brown v. Board of Education*, the school desegregation case. And that is one reason why opponents to abortion continue to push for a ban on the procedure. In *Roe v. Wade*, the 1973 case that established the right of a woman to choose abortion, seven of the justices joined the majority position. However, in subsequent rulings, the vote has been much closer—often 5 to 4—in upholding the abortion right.

Because the Court relies so heavily on precedent, separate opinions play a key role when lawyers attempt to change the law. In *Brown v. Board of Education*, the lawyers arguing for school desegregation quoted Justice John Marshall Harlan's stinging dissent in *Plessy v. Ferguson*, the 1896 case that cemented segregation in place for more than half a century. Harlan had proclaimed the constitution "color-blind," and insisted that "the arbitrary separation of citizens on the basis of race . . . cannot be justified upon any legal grounds." Even though his views did not influence the Court at the time to reverse its stand, Harlan's prestige and eloquence helped persuade a more liberal Court years later.

In some cases, concurring justices' statements can explain and even strengthen the position taken in the majority opinion. A concurring opinion can also sometimes establish guidelines for future courts. For example, in the Pentagon Papers case (*New York Times* v. *United States*), the Court by a 6 to 3 vote allowed the *Times* and the *Washington Post* to print the Pentagon Papers, a massive, classified report on U.S. involvement in Vietnam. The written decision in this monumental case consisted of a single page and was issued per curiam. Per curiam means "by the court." Such a decision is unsigned, short, and usually on noncontroversial subjects. In the case of the Pentagon Papers, the Court may have issued a per curiam opinion because there was little time to develop a more in-depth opinion that would meet the approval of all six justices supporting the decision.

In allowing publication of the report, the Court's ruling stated only that the government had failed to meet "the heavy burden of showing justification for the enforcement of such a [prior] restraint [on a free press]."

Two concurring opinions went much further in bolstering freedom of the press and setting a precedent that future courts would use. Justices Byron White and Potter Stewart accepted the government's claim that publication of the report could damage the nation's war efforts. Even so, the justices refused to allow the government to stop the presses. The First Amendment, they stated in their concurring opinions, protected freedom of the press even in this case. Justice White wrote that the government could override the First Amendment's protection of the press only when publication resulted "in direct, immediate, and irreparable harm to our Nation, or its people." White's words became the standard on which future courts relied when determining cases involving national security and the press.

A Monumental Victory

Champions of civil rights and free speech applauded the *Sullivan* decision. Alexander Meiklejohn, a noted advocate of free speech, commented that the *Sullivan* decision should be celebrated by "dancing in the streets." First Amendment scholar Harry Kalven Jr. of the University of Chicago Law School called the decision "the greatest First Amendment victory in Court history."

Others, though, were less enthusiastic about the decision. Some, like Robert M. Hutchins, university president and founder of the Center for the Study of Democratic Institutions, feared that Justice Brennan's majority opinion did not go far enough in protecting free speech. The decision, he said, left a large loophole by allowing juries to stop speech when malice could be proved. He favored the complete immunity from libel put forth in the concurring opinions.

In a roundtable discussion of the case shortly after the Court issued its ruling, Harry Ashmore, former Pulitzer Prize–winning editor of the *Arkansas Gazette*, worried that Southern juries would simply find malice in every case involving the criticism of race policies. "It's almost impossible to get a fair trial in the South if there is a racial issue involved," he said.

On the other side of the spectrum, public officials protested that the decision would make them a target of all kinds of unfair charges. California's attorney general, Stanley Mosk, was concerned that the decision might "hamper the operation of government" because good people would not want to expose themselves to unfair criticism by running for public office. Some in the South and elsewhere feared that polite discussion would be replaced by foul language and hateful speech because of the ruling.

During the two decades that followed, appeals courts reversed almost 70 percent of the libel judgments against

publishers. Without *Sullivan*'s "actual malice" standard,
the number of reversals would have been considerably
fewer and the national press may have been less willing to
cover controversial subjects. Without the vigorous
reporting of the national press, the American people might
not have known about the abuses against black citizens in
the South. Americans' revulsion at seeing adults attacking
schoolchildren helped force Congress to pass civil rights
laws on voting, housing, education, and other areas.

If Sullivan had been successful in his suit before the
Supreme Court, newspapers and television stations would
have faced an onslaught of similar suits awarding millions
in damages. Judge Alex Kozinski of the United States
Court of Appeals for the Ninth Circuit says the effect could
have been disastrous for the civil rights struggle and
would have threatened the survival of a free press. The
lawsuits, if successful, would have

> effectively [rung] down the curtain on conditions
> of blacks in the South, for every story and every
> advertisement commenting on those conditions
> would expose the media sources to liability.
> Worse, if L. B. Sullivan—a small-town official
> from the heart of Dixie—could intimidate the *New
> York Times*, the media in this country would
> become as effective as a toothless guard dog.

Without the *Sullivan* decision, the *New York Times*
might not have published the Pentagon Papers, and the
Washington Post might have toned down its pursuit of
the Watergate story that led to President Richard Nixon's
demise. "The rise of such investigative journalism would
not have been possible if the old law of libel had still
shielded officials from criticism," wrote Anthony Lewis
in his classic book on the *Sullivan* case, *Make No Law*.

WHEN IT IS CRIMINAL
TO SPEAK ONE'S MIND

In civil libel suits, like the *Sullivan* case, one person or entity sues another person or entity (a newspaper, for example) to collect damages. A jury can require a guilty party to pay for actual damages to the person who filed the suit. In addition, the jury can assess punitive damages. These can sometimes amount to millions of dollars and are designed to discourage the libeler and others from repeating the bad behavior.

In criminal libel cases, the state or federal government files charges against a person or entity. Criminal libel, unlike civil suits, often carries a jail sentence as well as a fine.

Eight months after the U.S. Supreme Court decided *Sullivan*, the justices imposed the same restrictions on criminal libel law that they had on civil libel law. The criminal case, *Garrison* v. *Louisiana*, involved controversial district attorney Jim Garrison of Louisiana. State courts convicted Garrison of criminal libel after he criticized New Orleans judges. He said during a news conference that the judges' refusal to approve funds for undercover agents raised "interesting questions about the racketeer influences on our eight vacation-minded judges." A judge sentenced Garrison to four months in jail and a $1,000 fine.

The Court overturned Garrison's conviction. Justice William J. Brennan Jr., author of the *Sullivan* decision, wrote the opinion. States could not use criminal libel laws to punish critics of government officials, Brennan wrote, unless they could prove that the statements had been "made with actual malice—that is, with knowledge that it was false or with reckless disregard of whether it was false or not."

While not ruling against criminal libel laws altogether, Brennan made it clear that such laws were outdated and probably no longer needed. "It can hardly be urged," he wrote, "that the maintenance of peace requires a criminal prosecution for private defamation."

As they had in the *Sullivan* case, Justices Hugo L. Black, William O. Douglas, and Arthur J. Goldberg strongly opposed restrictions on speech and called for a complete ban on criminal prosecutions for libel. "[T]here is absolutely no place in this country for the old, discredited English star chamber law of seditious criminal libel," Black wrote in his concurring opinion.

Since *Garrison*, there have been few prosecutions for criminal libel. Many states repealed such laws after the Court's decision on the matter. Still, criminal libel laws existed in seventeen states in 2005. Ken Paulson, executive director of the First Amendment Center, wants to see all criminal libel laws repealed. "There's no justification for keeping these laws on the books," he said. "A free society doesn't threaten citizens with jail for exercising their freedom of speech. If someone writes an article that is defamatory, a plaintiff can sue and recover monetary damages. The system works."

According to free-speech advocates, repeal of such laws is long overdue. "If we criminalize speech," said legal expert Randy Dryer, "half of the Founding Fathers would have been in prison" for criticizing government.

In several recent rulings, judges have reversed convictions and in some cases overturned state laws that impose jail time for insults. But in a few cases, higher courts have allowed the laws because they satisfy the "actual malice" rule required by the high court.

In 2004, the courts rejected Colorado police efforts to stop a college student from poking fun at a University of North Colorado professor. The student, Thomas Mink, included a photograph of finance professor Junius Peake in his satirical newsletter, *The Howling Pig*. Mink had retouched the photo to make Peake resemble rock star Gene Simmons, a member of the band KISS noted for his outrageous makeup. Peake reported the incident to Greeley, Colorado police, who seized Mink's computer and threatened to charge him under the state's criminal libel law. Passed in 1963, the law bans statements "tending to blacken the memory of one who is dead" or that "impeach the honesty, integrity, virtue, or reputation or expose the natural defects of one who is alive." If convicted, Mink could have been sentenced to jail.

A few days after the incident, the judge blocked the city's threatened prosecution of Mink and ordered the police to return his computer. "Even our colonialists of America engaged in this type of speech, with great lust and robustness," said U.S. District Judge Lewis Babcock in issuing his ruling. The judge denied Mink's attempt to overturn the state's criminal libel law, however. Mink, along with the American Civil Liberties Union of Colorado, filed suit asking a federal court to declare the law unconstitutional. The U.S. Court of Appeals in Denver heard arguments in Mink's suit on January 9, 2006. The case was still under advisement when this book went to print.

Other criminal libel laws have already been struck down in court or are waiting for a ruling. In Puerto Rico, a federal appeals court declared the law of that region unconstitutional because it ignored First Amendment protections. The case involved a news reporter who was sentenced to a jail term of up to three years for articles written about a police officer. In its ruling, the court noted that media reports about public officials lay "at the heart of the First Amendment." Puerto Rico's law was voided because it did not require prosecutors to prove the articles were written with "actual malice" and did not allow a dismissal if the information in the articles was true.

Utah's Supreme Court ruled that the state's criminal libel law violated the Constitution because it did not require similar safeguards. The ruling came about as a result of a student's arrest for referring to his principal as a "town drunk" on his personal Web site. The court said the law "infringes upon a substantial amount of constitutionally protected speech" and is "therefore overbroad and unconstitutional."

Another case, *Kansas* v. *Carson*, tested that state's criminal libel laws and lost. The case involved two Kansas newspapermen who suggested that a judge and another elected official did not live in the community as required by law. The rumor, reported in the January 2001 edition of *The New Observer*, a free, local publication, turned out to be false. Wyandotte County police charged the two men, publisher David W. Carson and editor Edward Powers, of violating the state's antidefamation law. The law calls for a $2,500 fine and up to a year in jail for violators. To win a conviction, prosecutors must prove that the offending material was published with "actual malice," as required by the Supreme Court.

Both men are former lawyers who were disbarred earlier for unprofessional behavior. On July 17, 2002, a jury of six convicted them of criminal libel, a misdemeanor. It was the first time in almost thirty years that a U.S. news organization was found guilty of criminal defamation. The men appealed to the Kansas State Supreme Court after being sentenced to fines and probation. In August 2004, that court issued a decision affirming the men's convictions.

"Reporters and editors would have held back from many stories if critical articles had been sure of escaping libel suits only when they were 'absolutely confirmable in every detail.'"

SUBSEQUENT PRESS CASES

Supreme Court decisions in the years following the *Sullivan* case have further defined the rights of a free press. The Court's decision in two joint cases, *Associated Press* v. *Walker* and *Curtis Publishing Company* v. *Butts*, extended *Sullivan*'s rules on libel to include public figures as well as public officials. Issued in 1967, the ruling required those in the public eye to prove malice in order to collect damages in a libel suit.

The Court used a 1968 decision in *St. Amant* v. *Thompson* to define "reckless disregard" in publishing libelous materials. Justice Byron R. White, writing for the Court, said "reckless conduct is not measured by whether a reasonably prudent man would have published, or would have investigated before publishing. There must be sufficient evidence to permit the conclusion that the defendant in fact entertained serious doubts as to the truth of his publication."

Libel rulings under a more conservative Court headed by Chief Justice Warren Burger—and later by Chief Justice William H. Rehnquist—sent mixed messages to the press and public. In a 1971 case, *Rosenbloom* v. *Metromedia, Inc.*, the Court made it more difficult for ordinary people to collect libel damages from the media. In the case, a radio station reported that a bookseller, Rosenbloom, had been arrested for selling obscene material. A jury later acquitted Rosenbloom of the charges. He sued the station for libel, claiming it had falsely accused him of being a "smut peddler." The Court ruled against Rosenbloom because he had not proved the station had intentionally

JUSTICE LEWIS F. POWELL JR. ESTABLISHED THE DEFINITION OF A PUBLIC
PERSON IN HIS OPINION IN *GERTZ* V. *ROBERT WELCH*.

tried to malign him. Private citizens who sued over statements concerning matters of public interest had to prove
malice to win their case, according to the ruling. Because
the public had a "vital interest" in the matter, the bookseller involved in the case fell under the same category as
public figures did.

Another decision three years later narrowed the definition of who was a public figure, making it easier for
ordinary citizens to collect damages. A narrow majority in
the 1974 case *Gertz* v. *Robert Welch* ruled that *Sullivan* did

not apply to private citizens who were not involved in far-reaching public matters. In his majority opinion, Justice Lewis F. Powell Jr. defined public figures as:

> those who . . . have assumed roles of especial prominence in the affairs of society. Some occupy positions of such persuasive power and influence that they are deemed public figures for all purposes. More commonly, those classed as public figures have thrust themselves to the forefront of particular public controversies in order to influence the resolution of the issues involved. In either event, they invite attention and comment.

Ordinary citizens, according to Powell, did not have access to the media and could not defend themselves as public figures and officials could. Nevertheless, ordinary citizens still had to prove negligence, but not actual malice, to collect compensatory damages from newspapers and other media. The ruling required a proof of malice, however, for punitive damages. Punitive damages are awarded to punish a defendant or to prevent him or her from repeating the offense. Compensatory damages cover only the actual cost of repairing the harm caused by an action.

The requirements were less stringent than those required of public figures and officials, but they were more than Justice White thought necessary. In a stinging dissent, White argued that ordinary citizens should have to prove only that a paper printed false statements about them that exposed them to contempt, hatred, or ridicule. They should not have to prove negligence, malice, or anything else, he said. The justice accused the Court of "scuttling the libel laws of the States" and "of deprecating the reputation interest of ordinary citizens and rendering them powerless to protect themselves."

Justices Brennan and Douglas dissented for reasons

opposite those of Justice White. As he had done in the
Sullivan case, Douglas objected to any restraints on
the press. In Douglas's view, the First Amendment barred
states from passing any libel law against the media. The
Gertz opinion, he said, eroded First Amendment rights to
free speech and press freedom.

Brennan opposed the ruling on the grounds that the
case involved discussion of public matters, "an alleged
conspiracy to discredit local police forces." The case
should have required proof of malice because of its connection to public issues, Brennan said. By not requiring
private citizens to prove malice, he added, the decision
did not give the press the "breathing space" essential to
fulfilling its role as watchdog.

Three other cases pared down the category of "public
figure" even more. In *Time, Inc.* v. *Firestone, Hutchinson* v.
Proxmire, and *Wolston* v. *Reader's Digest* the Court said
people could not be considered public figures merely
because they had been featured in the press.

The *Sullivan* ruling played a central role in several
other cases before the Court. Chief Justice Rehnquist's
conservative Court reduced the protections for those
expressing opinions in *Milkovich* v. *Lorain Journal Co.* Until
then, most courts had held that the First Amendment protected opinions, which were not judged false or true but
simply considered expression. In the 1990 case, the Court
ruled 7 to 2 that columns and other opinion pieces might
be libelous if they "impl[ied] an assertion of objective fact"
that was proved false. In writing the majority decision,
Chief Justice Rehnquist stated that the statement "In my
opinion John Jones is a liar" could do as much harm to a
person's reputation as "Jones is a liar." Justices William
Brennan and Thurgood Marshall dissented.

The Court again ruled against the press in a libel suit
in the 1991 case *Masson* v. *New Yorker Magazine.* In that

case, evidence showed that a reporter had altered quotations by psychoanalyst Jeffrey Masson in a magazine article. The magazine argued that the altered quotes were substantially true and because Masson was a public figure, he had to prove the magazine was guilty of actual malice. A unanimous Court ruled that the First Amendment did not protect the reporter's distortions. In his opinion for the Court, Justice Anthony Kennedy reconfirmed that the First Amendment limits libel suits by public figures like Masson. But, Kennedy wrote, such people can justifiably file suit if statements about them are a "gross distortion of truth." The justices agreed that the altered quotations in the case met that definition.

The Court firmly backed a free press in the 1988 case of *Hustler Magazine* v. *Falwell*. In that case, a unanimous Court ruled that the First Amendment protected satire, even when it was offensive. Fundamentalist minister Jerry Falwell claimed that a parody in the magazine defamed him, but the Court ruled that the satire could not reasonably be considered statements of actual facts.

Other Threats to a Free Press

The *Sullivan* ruling, however, cannot protect the media from other threats posed by libel suits. Monumental court costs have made it extremely expensive to defend against libel. Those costs and the fear of skyrocketing damage awards have forced some media companies to settle suits instead of pursuing them. In many cases, juries have shown their dislike for the press by awarding exorbitant damages to plaintiffs. The highest award to date totaled $222,720,000. The jury granted the award to MMAR Group, Inc., a Texas securities firm, after the company sued the *Wall Street Journal* over an article on a questionable investment deal. A court ordered a new trial when it was determined that MMAR had failed to turn over vital

Free speech online

The popularity of the Internet has raised difficult questions about what to do about libelous statements on the Web. With new technologies in communication, one person can send out statements that can be read within minutes by readers throughout the world. This greatly expands the ability of ordinary people to publicize their views. But it also opens the door to libelers who would use the Internet to malign their enemies.

"The Internet breathes life into the First Amendment by ensuring more people the opportunity to speak out on matters of public importance," says First Amendment lawyer David L. Hudson Jr., "but it also affords greater opportunity for individuals . . . to defame others."

Courts are now being asked to determine how libel laws apply to the Internet. In 1998 the U.S. Supreme Court let stand a federal court's decision on an Internet case. The decision in the case, *Zeran* v. *America Online*, protected Internet providers from libel claims for statements made by their clients. Kenneth Zeran sued America Online after an unidentified AOL user put an ad on an AOL bulletin board that offered joke items related to the Oklahoma City bombing. The ad told interested buyers to contact Zeran and gave his first name and telephone number. At Zeran's request, AOL deleted the posting and a second one that appeared. As a result of the hoax, Zeran received complaints and death threats. He sued AOL for damages. The District Court, upheld by the federal appeals court, ruled that Internet providers could not be held responsible for statements posted by their clients unless the providers controlled what appeared on the site. The ruling cited a 1996 law passed by Congress, the Communications Decency Act, which says that "no provider or user of an interactive computer service shall be treated as the publisher or speaker of any information provided by another information content provider."

Individuals who post material on the Web, however, may face libel charges. In the case of Thomas Mink, police seized a computer and threatened prosecution for criminal libel because of a publication he posted on the Internet. Police got a court order to look at all e-mails, including those sent by readers, and other Web records relating to *The Howling Pig*, Mink's satirical publication. Mink and the Colorado branch of the American Civil Liberties Union have filed suit in federal court, claiming that the police violated the Electronic Communications Privacy Act when they reviewed the e-mails. Allowing police access to e-mails, the suit contends, violated Mink's Fourth Amendment rights against unreasonable search and seizure and the Privacy Protection Act of 1980. The hearing in the case has been scheduled in 2006.

Recent federal antiterrorism legislation has also produced court challenges to government access to Internet communications. Congress passed the USA PATRIOT Act (officially, the Uniting and Strengthening America by Providing Appropriate Tools Required to Intercept and Obstruct Terrorism Act) in 2001 in response to the September 11 terrorist attacks in New York City and Washington, D.C. It gives the government broad powers to monitor a person's Web records and get access to Internet service providers' records.

In 2004, a federal court put limits on the government's power to spy on Internet users under the PATRIOT Act. The ruling in the case, *Doe* v. *Gonzalez*, barred the use of secret subpoenas, issued by the Federal Bureau of Investigation without court approval. Government officials in the *Doe* case tried to force a library to turn over billing information, access logs, and other information about a library patron's online activities. Library officials were not allowed to tell the patron of the government's actions. The court ruled that such gag orders violated the free-speech rights of the library.

One problem posed by Internet cases is the question of jurisdiction. "The international reach of online communications now transforms such jurisdictional questions into global issues of competing international law," notes attorney Hudson. The courts, he says, will have to clarify how current laws will handle that and other thorny issues. In reviewing Internet cases, though, free-speech advocates hope courts will continue *Sullivan*'s legacy of tolerance when it comes to free speech. "We can hope that courts will recognize, as the Supreme Court did 25 years ago in *New York Times* v. *Sullivan*, that 'erroneous statement is inevitable in free debate,'" Hudson said.

evidence. Before a new trial could be held, MMAR withdrew its suit against the newspaper.

According to the Libel Defense Resource Center, newspapers and other news outlets win more than nine of every ten libel suits filed against them. But in 83 percent of the suits filed, the jury first ruled against the media and a court subsequently overruled the verdict. Even when they win, media outlets can face million-dollar attorney fees and court costs. Anthony Lewis, in *Make No Law*, describes the "chilling" effect such expenses can have on the press. He relates the case of the Alton, Illinois, *Telegraph*, noted for its investigative stories about local government. The paper had to settle a libel suit brought by a local builder when it could not put up a $10 million bond required to meet the costs of an appeal. After paying a $1.4 million settlement, the newspaper avoided reporting on official misdeeds because it feared another costly lawsuit, Lewis wrote. A few states have begun to adopt rules to reduce the number of frivolous cases filed against the press.

Some media critics believe that the *Sullivan* ruling has encouraged inaccurate reporting. They say that irresponsible reporting is partly to blame for the increase in libel suits against the press. By alienating the public, malicious reports turn people—and juries—against the press and threaten the freedom of all news media. Journalist George A. Krimsky notes that citizens depend on a free press to help them govern. The press keeps them informed about their government so that they can make intelligent decisions at the ballot box. As democracy's watchdog, he says, the press has a responsibility to take that job seriously. "There is nothing in the American constitution that says the press must be responsible and accountable. Those requirements were reserved for government," Krimsky notes. But, he adds, "There is still a need today—perhaps more than ever—for identifying sense amidst the nonsense, for sifting the important from the trivial, and, yes, for telling the truth. Those goals still constitute the best mandate for a free press in a democracy."

In the 1990s, lower courts of appeal issued several decisions that held journalists accountable for illegal acts committed while pursuing a story. The courts ruled that journalists had no First Amendment privilege to lie or violate the law. In one case, the appeals court found a journalist guilty of "misrepresentation amounting to fraud" when she used a hidden camera to record activities at a Minnesota care facility. Advocates for press freedom say that such rulings are troubling because they interfere with reporters' ability to do their job. The Supreme Court has not ruled on the issue of reporters' illegal activities. But in the 2001 case *Bartnicki et al.* v. *Vopper*, the high court ruled that the First Amendment protected a radio commentator's right to play a recording of a cell phone conversation recorded illegally by someone else. The Court based its decision in part on Justice Brennan's admonition in *Sullivan* that "debate on public issues should be uninhibited, robust, and wide open."

Conflicts continue to erupt over the role of the press and the extent of its freedoms. Even so, forty years after the *Sullivan* ruling, the case remains a monument to the First Amendment and the importance of free speech and the press in a democracy. In *Sullivan*, media ethics professor Jane E. Kirtley notes, "the Supreme Court recognized that, in order to guarantee an informed electorate, the news media must be protected, given 'breathing space,' granted the right to be wrong."

Legal expert Ellen K. Solender goes far beyond press freedom in her assessment of the case. "*New York Times* v. *Sullivan* was not just a victory for the First Amendment; it was a victory for all civil rights. That's what it's all about. Free speech, free press are fundamental to all freedom."

notes

Introduction

p. 7, par. 1, "Heed Their Rising Voices," *New York Times* (March 29, 1960), p. L25.

Sidebar

p. 9, Gary A. Paranzino, "The Future of Libel Law and Independent Appellate Review: Making Sense of *Bose Corp. v. Consumers Union of United States, Inc.*," *Cornell Law Review* (1985). http://paranzino.com/libel.html
Ronald K. L. Collins, "*New York Times Co.* v. *Sullivan*: The Case that Changed First Amendment History," First Amendment Center (March 2004). http://catalog.freedom forum.org/SpecialTopics/NYTSullivan/summary.html

p. 10, par. 1–3, *New York Times* v. *Sullivan*, 376 U.S. 254 (1964).
p. 10, par. 4–5, Ellen K. Solender, "What If," *Communications Lawyer* (Summer, 1984), cited in Times *v.* Sullivan *and the Civil Rights Movement* by Lynne Flocke, S. I. Newhouse School of Public Communications, Syracuse University. http://civilrightsandthepress.syr.edu/reflection.html
p. 10, par. 6, Rodney A. Smolla, *Suing the Press: Libel, the Media and Power* (Oxford University Press, 1986), cited in Times *v.* Sullivan *and the Civil Rights Movement* by Lynne Flocke.

Chapter 1

p. 14, par. 4, "Aid for Dr. King Urged; 3 Leading Clergymen Here Open Drive for Funds," *New York Times* (February 26, 1960), p. 8.

p. 15, par. 2–p. 18, par. 2, "Heed Their Rising Voices," *New York Times* (March 29, 1960), p. L25.

p. 18, par. 3, *New York Times* v. *Sullivan*, 376 U.S. 254 (1964).

p. 18, par. 4, Brief for the Petitioner, *New York Times* v. *Sullivan*, 376 U.S. 254 (1964), pp. 17, 26, 66.

p. 19, par. 1, Anthony Lewis, *Make No Law: The Sullivan Case and the First Amendment* (New York: Random House, 1991), p. 7.

p. 19, par. 2–3, Newhouse Civil Rights and the Press Symposium, "Opening the School House Door: Brown and Its Aftermath" (Syracuse University, April 24, 2004), tape 2. http://civilrightsandthepress.syr.edu/transcripts.html

p. 20, par. 1, Transcript of proceedings on merits, November 1, 2, and 3, 1960, Circuit Court of Montgomery, *New York Times* v. *Sullivan*, 376 U.S. 254 (1964).

p. 21, par. 2, Kermit L. Hall, "Cultural History and the First Amendment: *New York Times* v. *Sullivan* and its Times," *Constitutionalism and American Culture: Writing the New Constitutional History*, eds. Sandra F. VanBurkleo, Kermit L. Hall, and Robert J. Kaczorowski (Lawrence: University Press of Kansas, 2002).

p. 22, par.1, Lewis, *Make No Law*, p. 13.

p. 22, par. 4, *New York Times* v. *Sullivan*, 376 U.S. 254 (1964).

p. 24, par. 3, "Times Retracts Statement in Ad; Acts on Protest of Alabama Governor over Assertions in Segregation Matter," *New York Times* (May 16, 1960), p. 22.

p. 24, par. 5–p. 25, par. 2, Transcript of proceedings, *New York Times* v. *Sullivan*.

p. 25, par. 3, "Alabama Governor Sues for $1,000,000," *New York Times* (May 31, 1960), p. 20.

Chapter 2

p. 28, par. 2, Claude Sitton, "Dr. King Is Seized in Tax Indictment; Atlanta Acts on Alabama's Request—Negro Leader to Fight Extradition," *New York Times* (February 18, 1960), p. 14.

p. 28, par. 3, "Dr. King Paid Taxes in Alabama Dispute," *New York Times* (February 25, 1960), p. 14.

p. 28, par. 5, "President Urged to Act in South; Dr. King Asks Intervention to Stop Police 'Terror' in Montgomery Protests," *New York Times* (March 10, 1960), p. 25.

p. 29, par. 1, "Dr. King Favors Buyers' Boycott; National Campaign a Must, Negro Leader Says at Sit-In Strategy Talks," *New York Times* (April 16, 1960), p. 15.

p. 29, par. 1, Allan Knight Chalmers, "Sit-in Protests Hailed; Demonstrations Declared Result of Joint and Directed Efforts," *New York Times* (April 26, 1960), p. 36.

p. 31, par. 2–3, "Dr. King Acquitted of Perjury on Tax," *New York Times* (May 29, 1960), p. 1.

p. 31, par. 4, Anthony Lewis, *Make No Law: The Sullivan Case and the First Amendment* (New York: Random House, 1991).

Chapter 3

p. 33, par. 2, Robert Friedman, "Freedom of the Press: How Far Can They Go?" *American Heritage*, 33:6 (October/ November, 1982), pp. 1, 16.

p. 34, par. 2, Walter B. Jones, "Memories of John Brown," *Montgomery Advertiser*, August 7, 1950.

p. 35, par. 1, Anthony Lewis, "Thoughts That We Hate," 1994 Knight Lecture, Stanford University (1994).

p. 35, par. 3, Transcript of proceedings on merits, November 1, 2, and 3, 1960, Circuit Court of Montgomery, *New York Times* v. *Sullivan*, 376 U.S. 254 (1964).

p. 36, par. 2, Mary Ellen Maatman, "Working the Devil in the Law of the Land," Widener University School of Law, Paper 786 (2005), pp. 77–78.

p. 37, par. 2–p. 38, par. 2, Transcript of proceedings on merits, November 1, 2, and 3, 1960.

p. 38, par. 3, Newhouse Civil Rights and the Press Symposium, "Opening the School House Door: Brown and Its Aftermath," (Syracuse University, April 24, 2004), tape 2. http://civilrightsandthepress.syr.edu/transcripts.html

Sidebar

pp. 39–41, The Supreme Court Historical Society http://www.supremecourthistory.org

Administrative Office of the U.S. Courts
http://www.uscourts.gov
Iowa Court Information System
http://www.judicial.state.ia.us/students/6
There is also a diagram on the last Web site.

p. 42, par. 1, "Alabama Justice," *Time*, April 7, 1961, Press section.

Chapter 4

p. 43, par. 1, "Eighteenth-Century American Newspapers in the Library of Congress: Massachusetts, Boston," No. 200, *Publick Occurrences Both Forreign and Domestick* (September 25, 1690). http://www.loc.gov/rr/news/18th/200.html

p. 45, par. 3–4, David Sloan, "John Campbell and the *Boston News-Letter*," The Early America Review (2004) http://earlyamerica.com/review/2005_winter_spring/john_campbell.htm

p. 47, par. 2, "History of Press Freedom," *Illinois Press Association Guide to First Amendment and Illinois Access Laws* (1995). http://www.illinoisfirstamendmentcenter.com/freedom_press_history.php

p. 47, par. 3, Thomas Paine, *Common Sense* (Philadelphia: W. & T. Bradford, 1776). http://www.ushistory.org/paine/commonsense/sense1.htm

p. 47, par. 3, Robert G. Ingersoll, "Thomas Paine, 1892," *The Works of Robert G. Ingersoll* (Louisville, KY: 1892) http://www.infidels.org/library/historical/robert_ingersoll/thomas_paine.html

p. 48, par. 1, "Thomas Jefferson: Establishing a Federal Republic," Library of Congress (Washington, DC: 2001). http://www.loc.gov/exhibits/jefferson/jefffed.html

p. 48, par. 3–p.49, par. 2, Constitutional Rights Foundation, "The Alien and Sedition Acts: Defining American Freedom," *Bill of Rights in Action*, 19:4 (Fall 2001). http://www.crf-usa.org/bria/bria19_4b.htm

p. 49, par. 3, "The Alien and Sedition Acts of 1798," from Folwell's *Laws of the U.S.*, Archiving Early America. http://earlyamerica.com/earlyamerica/milestones/sedition

p. 49, par. 4, Senate Commission on Protecting and Reducing Government Secrecy, *Secrecy: A Brief Account of the American Experience* (1997), Senate Document, p. A-57.

p. 50, par. 2–3, *Schenck* v. *United States*, 249 U.S. 47 (1919).

p. 50, par. 5–p. 52, par. 2, *Near* v. *Minnesota*, 283 U.S. 697, 1931.

p. 52, par. 5, Robert Friedman, "Freedom of the Press: How Far Can They Go?" *American Heritage* 33:6 (October/November 1982), pp. 1, 16.

p. 53, par. 3–p. 54, par. 2, *Chaplinsky* v. *New Hampshire*, 315 U.S. 568, 571–572 (1942).

p. 54, par. 3–p. 55, par. 1, *Beauharnais* v. *Illinois*, 343 U.S. 250 (1952).

p. 55, par. 2–p. 56, par. 1, *Konigsberg* v. *State Bar of California*, 366 U.S. 36, 49 (1961).

p. 56, par. 2, *Terminiello* v. *Chicago*, 337 U.S. 1 (1949).

p. 56, par. 3–p. 57, par. 2, *Roth* v. *United States*, 354 U.S. 476 (1957).

Sidebar

pp. 58–63, "Bill of Rights in Action," Constitutional Rights Foundation,7: 4 (Spring 1991). http://www.crf-usa.org/bria/bria7_4.htm#second
Fourteenth Amendment, U.S. Constitution.
"The Fourteenth Amendment," The Library of Congress. http://memory.loc.gov/ammem/today/jul28.html
Gitlow v. *New York*, 268 U.S. 652 (1925).
Oyez, U.S. Supreme Court Multimedia site. *Gitlow* v. *New York*. http://www.oyez.org/oyez/resource/case/140
Permoli v. *Municipality No. 1 of City of New Orleans*, 44 U.S. 589 (1845).
Slaughterhouse Cases, 83 U.S. 36 (1872).

Chapter 5

p. 63, par. 1, Louis Henkin, "Herbert Wechsler," *Proceedings of the American Philosophical Society*, 146:3 (September 2002), pp. 311–316.

p. 63, par. 4–p. 65, par. 4, Transcript of records, Alabama

Supreme Court, *New York Times* v. *Sullivan*, 376 U.S. 254 (1964).

p. 67, par. 4–p. 73, par. 2, Brief for the Petitioner, *New York Times* v. *Sullivan*, 376 U.S. 254 (1964).

p. 69, par. 2, *Bridges* v. *California*, cited in Brief for the Petitioner, *New York Times* v. *Sullivan*.

p. 69, par. 4, *Cantwell* v. *Connecticut*, cited in Brief for the Petitioner, *New York Times* v. *Sullivan*.

p. 70, par. 3–4, Sedition Act of 1798, cited in Brief for the Petitioner, *New York Times* v. *Sullivan*.

p. 71, par. 4, *Pennekamp* v. *Florida*, cited in Brief for the Petitioner, *New York Times* v. *Sullivan*.

p. 73, par. 3, Brief for the Petitioner, *Abernathy et al.* v. *Sullivan*, 376 U.S. 254 (1964).

p. 73, par. 4, Anthony Lewis, *Make No Law: The Sullivan Case and the First Amendment* (New York: Random House, 1991), p. 245.

p. 73, par. 5–p. 77, par. 2, Brief for the Respondent, *New York Times* v. *Sullivan*.

p. 74, par. 2, Thomas Jefferson, cited in Brief for the Respondent, *New York Times* v. *Sullivan*.

p. 74, par. 4–p. 75, par. 2, William Howard Taft, cited in Brief for the Respondent, *New York Times* v. *Sullivan*.

p. 77, par. 1, Seventh Amendment, U.S. Constitution.

p. 77, par. 4, *Amicus curiae* brief of the *Chicago Tribune*, *New York Times* v. *Sullivan*, pp. 7–8.

p. 77, par. 5, *Amicus curiae* brief of the *Washington Post*, *New York Times* v. *Sullivan*.

p. 78, par. 1, Lewis, *Make No Law*, p. 36.

p. 78, par. 2, *Amicus curiae* brief of the American Civil Liberties Union, *New York Times* v. *Sullivan*, cited in Lewis, *Make No Law*, p. 126.

Chapter 6

p. 79, par. 1, Supreme Court Historical Society. Booklet on the U.S. Supreme Court.

p. 81, par. 2–p. 86, par. 3, Oral arguments (Herbert Wechsler), *New York Times* v. *Sullivan*, 376 U.S. 254 (1964).

p. 86, par. 4–p. 89, par. 3, Oral arguments (M. Roland
Nachman), *New York Times* v. *Sullivan*.

p. 89, par. 5–90, par. 1, Anthony Lewis, *Make No Law: The
Sullivan Case and the First Amendment* (New York: Random
House, 1991), pp. 118–119.

Chapter 7

p. 91, par. 3, Anthony Lewis, *Make No Law: The Sullivan Case and
the First Amendment* (New York: Random House, 1991), p.
181.

p. 93, par. 1–p. 97, par. 3, *New York Times* v. *Sullivan*, 376 U.S.
254 (1964).

p. 97, par. 5–p. 99, par. 1, Hugo L. Black, concurrence, *New
York Times* v. *Sullivan*.

p. 100, par. 1–4, Arthur J. Goldberg, concurrence, *New York
Times* v. *Sullivan*.

Sidebar

p. 102, par. 2, Richard Kluger, *Simple Justice* (New York: Alfred
A. Knopf, 1976), p. 706.

p. 102, par. 3, John Marshall Harlan, dissent, *Plessy* v. *Ferguson*,
163 U.S. 537 (1896).

p. 103, par. 1, David Rudenstine, *The Day the Presses Stopped*
(Berkeley: University of California Press, 1996), p. 301.

p. 103, par. 2, *New York Times* v. *United States*, 403 U.S. 713
(1971).

p. 103, par. 3, The National Security Archive, "The Pentagon
Papers: Secrets, Lies and Audiotapes (The Nixon Tapes and
the Supreme Court Tape)." http://www.gwu.edu/~nsarchiv/
NSAEBB/NSAEBB48/supreme.html

p. 104, par. 1, The Center for the Study of Democratic
Institutions Audio Archive, Program 124: *Freedom of the
Press—II*, moderated by Harry Kalven Jr.; tape numbers
A7684/R7, A7685/R7 (July 27, 1964). http://www.library.
ucsb.edu/speccoll/csdi/a7684.html

p. 104, par. 2–4, The Center for the Study of Democratic
Institutions Audio Archive, Program 123: *Freedom of the*

Press—I, moderated by Robert M. Hutchins; tape numbers A7682/R7, A7683/R7 (May 12, 1964). http://www.library. ucsb.edu/speccoll/csdi/a7682.html

p. 104, par. 5, *Amicus curiae* brief of *New York Times Co. et al.*, *Bose Corp.* v. *Consumers Union of United States, Inc.*, 466 U.S. 485 (1984). Cited in Gary A. Paranzino, "The Future of Libel Law and Independent Appellate Review: Making Sense of *Bose Corp.* v. *Consumers Union of United States, Inc.*," *Cornell Law Review* (1985).

p. 105, par. 2–3, Alex Kozinski, "The Bulwark Brennan Built," *Columbia Journalism Review* 30:4 (November 1, 1991), pp. 1–6.

p. 105, par. 4, Lewis, *Make No Law*, p. 158.

Sidebar

p. 106, par. 3–p. 107, par. 1, *Garrison* v. *Louisiana*, 379 U.S. 64 (1964).

p. 107, par. 2, Hugo L. Black, concurrence, *Garrison* v. *Louisiana*, 379 U.S. 64 (1964).

p. 107, par. 3, Ken Paulson, "Jailed for speech: Criminal libel is an old—and bad—idea," First Amendment Center (January 18, 2004). http://www.firstamendmentcenter.org/ commentary.aspx?id=12468

p. 107, par. 4, Bob Bernick Jr., "Salt Lake Demo pushing to repeal criminal slander and libel law," *Deseret Morning News* (October 19, 2005).

p. 107, par. 6–p. 108, par. 2, ACLU of Colorado, "ACLU Names Colorado Attorney General as Defendant in Challenge to Criminal Libel Statute and Settles Claims Against City of Greeley" (February 19, 2004). http://www.aclu.org/free speech/gen/10968prs20040219.html

p. 108, par. 2, Doyle Murphy, "Organizations join to readdress *Howling Pig* case," *Greeley Tribune* (April 5, 2005). http:// www.greeleytrib.com/article/20050405/NEWS/104050057 &SearchID=7321634576457

p. 108, par. 3, Barbara Wartelle Wall, "Legal Watch: Puerto Rico's Criminal Libel Law Declared Unconstitutional," Gannett News Watch. http://www.gannett.com/go/ newswatch/2003/february/nw0214-4.htm

p. 109, par. 2, "Utah court rejects criminal libel statute; says 'actual malice,' falsity necessary," *SPLC Report* 24:1 (Winter, 2002–2003), p. 31.

p. 109, par. 3, Center for Individual Freedom, "Extra! Extra! Kansas City Newspaper Convicted of Criminal Defamation," (August 1, 2002). http://www.cfif.org/htdocs/legalissues/legal_ updates/first_amendment_cases/criminal_ defamation.htm

p. 109, par. 3–4, John W. Dean, "An Extremely Rare Criminal Libel Case, Currently Proceeding in Kansas, Raises the Question Whether Libel Should Ever Be Prosecuted," FindLaw's Legal Commentary (December 6, 2002). http://writ.news.findlaw.com/dean/20021206.html

p. 110, par. 1, Lewis, *Make No Law*, p. 158.

p. 110, par. 3, *St. Amant* v. *Thompson*, 390 U.S. 727 (1968).

p. 110, par. 4, *Rosenbloom* v. *Metromedia, Inc.*, 403 U.S. 29 (1971).

p. 112, par. 2, *Gertz* v. *Robert Welch*, 418 U.S. 323 (1974).

p. 112, par. 4, Byron R. White, dissent, *Gertz* v. *Robert Welch*.

p. 113, par. 2, William J. Brennan Jr., dissent, *Gertz* v. *Robert Welch*.

p. 113, par. 4, *Milkovich* v. *Lorain Journal*, 497 U.S. 1 (1990).

p. 114, par. 1, *Masson* v. *New Yorker Magazine*, 501 U.S. 496 (1991).

p. 114, par. 1, Media Law Resource Center, "Frequently Asked Media Law Questions," New York (2005). http://www.medialaw.org

Sidebar

p. 115, par. 2, "ACLU Names Colorado Attorney General as Defendant in Challenge to Criminal Libel Statute and Settles Claims Against City of Greeley," American Civil Liberties of Colorado press release, February 19, 2004. http://www.aclu.org/freespeech/gen/10968prs20040219.html

p. 115, par. 2, David L. Hudson Jr., "Online Publishing Forces Evolution of Defamation Law," First Amendment Center (May 12, 1999). http://www.fac.org/analysis.aspx?id=10479

p. 115, par. 3, *Zeran* v. *America Online, Inc.*, 129 F.3d 327 (4th Cir. 1997).

p. 115, par. 3, Student Press Law Center, "Know Your Cybershield: Federal law offers online publishers protection from liability denied to their print counterparts," (2000). http://www.splc.org/legalresearch.asp?id=24

p. 116, par. 4, Electronic Frontier Foundation. http://www.eff.org

p. 117, par. 2, David L. Hudson Jr., "Online Publishing Forces Evolution of Defamation Law."

p. 118, par. 2, "Of Reputations and Reporters: A Conference Considers Better Protection for Journalists," *Time* (March 19, 1984). http://www.time.com/time/archive/preview/0,10987,950055,00.html

p. 118, par. 2, Lewis, *Make No Law*, p. 202.

p. 118, par. 2, Terry Francke, "Human Rights: Press Rights, Human Rights, and Cryptocracy," American Bar Association. http://www.abanet.org/irr/hr/fall01/francke.html

p. 118, par. 3, Chelsea DeWeese, "Lawyer v. Journalist: Debate at UM recognizes landmark libel case," The School of Journalism at the University of Montana (November 2004). http://www.umt.edu/journalism/news_pages/archives/November/Nov04/supco.htm

p. 118, par. 3, George A. Krimsky, "The Role of the Media in a Democracy," United States Information Agency. http://usinfo.org/media/press/essay3.htm

p. 119, par. 3, Jane E. Kirtley, "It's the Process, Stupid: Newsgathering Is the New Target," *Columbia Journalism Review* (September/October 2000). http://archives.cjr.org/year/00/3/kirtley.asp

p. 119, par. 4, Ellen K. Solender, "What If" in *Communications Lawyer* (Summer, 1984). Cited in Times *v.* Sullivan *and the Civil Rights Movement* by Lynne Flocke, S. I. Newhouse School of Public Communications, Syracuse University (2003). http://civilrightsandthepress.syr.edu/reflection.html

(All Web sites accessible as of November 8, 2005.)

Further Information

BOOKS

Cornelius, Kay. *The Supreme Court*. (Your Government: How It Works.) Broomall, PA: Chelsea House Publishers, 2000.

Cornwell, Nancy C. *Freedom of the Press: Rights and Liberties under the Law*. (America's Freedoms.) Santa Barbara: ABC-CLIO, 2004.

Egendorf, Laura K. *Censorship*. (Examining Issues Through Political Cartoons.) San Diego: Greenhaven Press, 2003.

Farish, Leah. *The First Amendment: Freedom of Speech, Religion, and the Press*. Berkeley Heights, NJ: Enslow Publishers, 1998.

Fireside, Harvey. *New York Times v. Sullivan: Affirming Freedom of the Press*. (Landmark Supreme Court Cases.) Berkeley Heights, NJ: Enslow Publishers, 1999.

Heath, David, and Charlotte Wilcox. *The Supreme Court of the United States*. (American Civics.) Mankato, MN: Bridgestone Books, 1999.

Hebert, David L., ed. *Freedom of the Press*. (Bill of Rights.) San Diego: Greenhaven Press, 2005.

Irons, Peter. *People's History of the Supreme Court*. New York: Penguin, 2000.

LeVert, Suzanne. *The Supreme Court*. New York: Benchmark Books, 2002.

Lewis, Anthony. *Make No Law: The Sullivan Case and the First Amendment*. New York: Random House, 1991.

McGlone, Catherine. *New York Times v. Sullivan and the Freedom of the Press Debate*. (Debating Supreme Court Decisions.) Berkeley Heights, NJ: Enslow Publishers, 2005.

Patrick, John J. *The Supreme Court of the United States: A Student Companion*, 2nd ed. (Oxford Student Companions to American Government). New York: Oxford University Press Children's Books, 2002.

Sanders, Mark C. *Supreme Court*. (American Government Today Series.) Austin, TX: Raintree/Steck-Vaughn Publishers, 2001.

Zeinert, Karen. *Free Speech: From Newspapers to Music Lyrics*. (Issues in Focus.) Berkeley Heights, NJ: Enslow Publishers, 1995.

AUDIO/VIDEO

The Center for the Study of Democratic Institutions Audio Archive, Program 89: *The First Amendment: Libel and Slander*. Moderated by Harry Kalven Jr.; tape numbers A7684/R7 (July 31, 1963). http://www.library.ucsb.edu/speccoll/csdi/a7626.html

_____. Program 123: *Freedom of the Press—I*. Moderated by Robert M. Hutchins; tape numbers A7682/R7, A7683/R7 (May 12, 1964).

_____. Program 124: *Freedom of the Press—II*. Moderated by Harry Kalven Jr.; tape numbers A7684/R7, A7685/R7 (July 27, 1964).

Irons, Peter, ed. *May It Please the Court: Courts, Kids, and the Constitution*. New York: The New York Press, 2000. Live recordings and transcripts of the Supreme Court oral arguments (audio).

Just The Facts—The United States Bill of Rights and Constitutional Amendments. (Just the Facts series.) Camarillo, CA: Goldhil Home Media I, 2004 (video).

Oral Arguments, *New York Times v. Sullivan*, 376 U.S. 254 (1964), Docket No. 39. http://www.oyez.org/oyez/resource/case/277/audioresources

Profiles of Freedom: A Living Bill of Rights. Arlington, VA: Bill of Rights Institute, 1997 (video).

WEB SITES

American Civil Liberties Union.
   http://www.aclu.org
Electronic Frontier Foundation.
   http://www.eff.org
FindLaw (U.S. Supreme Court Cases).
   http://www.findlaw.com/casecode/supreme.html
First Amendment Center.
   http://www.firstamendmentcenter.org
Freedom Forum.
   http://www.freedomforum.org
Landmark Cases of the U.S. Supreme Court.
   http://www.landmarkcases.org
Legal Information Institute, Cornell Law School.
   http://www.law.cornell.edu
Northwestern University, "Heed Their Rising Voices" ad.
   http://faculty-web.at.northwestern.edu/commstud/
   freespeech/cont/cases/nytsullivan1.html
Oyez Project, U.S. Supreme Court Multimedia Web site.
   http://www.oyez.org/oyez/frontpage
Reporters Committee for Freedom of the Press.
   http://www.rcfp.org
Student Press Law Center
   http://www.splc.org
Supreme Court of the United States.
   http://www.supremecourtus.gov
Supreme Court Historical Society.
   http://www.supremecourthistory.org

(All Web sites accessible as of November 8, 2005.)

BIBLIOGraPHY

ARTICLES

"Aid for Dr. King Urged; 3 Leading Clergymen Here Open Drive for Funds," *New York Times*, February 26, 1960, p. 8.

"Alabama Governor Sues for $1,000,000," *New York Times*, May 31, 1960, p. 20.

"Alabama Justice," *Time* (April 7, 1961), Press section.

"The Alien and Sedition Acts of 1798," Folwell's *Laws of the U.S.* http://earlyamerica.com/earlyamerica/milestones/sedition

American Civil Liberties Union of Colorado. "ACLU Names Colorado Attorney General as Defendant in Challenge to Criminal Libel Statute and Settles Claims Against City of Greeley" (February 19, 2004). http://www.aclu.org/freespeech/gen/10968prs20040219.html

Bernick, Bob Jr. "Salt Lake Demo pushing to repeal criminal slander and libel law," *Deseret Morning News*, October 19, 2005.

Center for Individual Freedom. "Extra! Extra! Kansas City Newspaper Convicted of Criminal Defamation" (August 1, 2002). http://www.cfif.org/htdocs/legal_issues/legal_updates/first_amendment_cases/criminal_defamation.htm

Chalmers, Allan Knight. "Sit-in Protests Hailed; Demonstrations Declared Result of Joint and Directed Efforts," *New York Times*, April 26, 1960, p. 36.

Clayton, James. "Right to Criticize Public Officials Upheld in High Court Libel Ruling," *Washington Post*, March 10, 1964, p. 1-A.

Collins, Ronald K. L. "*New York Times Co.* v. *Sullivan*: The Case that Changed First Amendment History," First Amendment Center (March 2004). http://catalog.freedom forum.org/SpecialTopics/NYTSullivan/summary.html

Constitutional Rights Foundation, "The Alien and Sedition Acts: Defining American Freedom," *Bill of Rights in Action*, 19:4 (Fall 2001). http://www.crf-usa.org/bria/bria19_4b.htm
____. "Bill of Rights in Action," 7:4 (Spring 1991). http://www.crf-usa.org/bria/bria19_4.htm

Dean, John W. "An Extremely Rare Criminal Libel Case, Currently Proceeding in Kansas, Raises the Question Whether Libel Should Ever Be Prosecuted," FindLaw's Legal Commentary (December 6, 2002). http://writ.news.findlaw.com/dean/20021206.html

DeWeese, Chelsea. "Lawyer v. Journalist: Debate at UM recognizes landmark libel case," The School of Journalism at the University of Montana (November 2004). http://www.umt.edu/journalism/news_pages/archives/November/Nov04/supco.htm

"Dr. King Acquitted of Perjury on Tax," *New York Times*, May 29, 1960, p. 1.

"Dr. King Favors Buyers' Boycott; National Campaign a Must, Negro Leader Says at Sit-In Strategy Talks," *New York Times*, April 16, 1960, p. 15.

"Dr. King Paid Taxes in Alabama Dispute," *New York Times*, February 25, 1960, p. 14.

"Eighteenth-Century American Newspapers in the Library of Congress: Massachusetts, Boston," No. 200, *Publick Occurrences Both Forreign and Domestick* (September 25, 1690). http://www.loc.gov/rr/news/18th/200.html

Flocke, Lynne. Times *v.* Sullivan *and the Civil Rights Movement*. S. I. Newhouse School of Public Communications, Syracuse University (2003). http://civilrightsandthepress.syr.edu/reflection.html

Francke, Terry. "Human Rights: Press Rights, Human Rights, and Cryptocracy," American Bar Association. http://www.abanet.org/irr/hr/fall01/francke.html

Friedman, Robert. "Freedom of the Press: How Far Can They

Go?" *American Heritage*, 33:6 (October/November, 1982),
pp. 1, 16.

Grant, Michael. "Watchdog Role of Press More Important
Than Ever," *Voice of San Diego*, September 29, 2005.

Hall, Kermit. "Cultural History & the First Amendment: *New
York Times* v. *Sullivan* & Its Times," *Constitutionalism &
American Culture: Writing the New Constitutional History*, ed.
Sandra F. Vanburkleo, et al. Lawrence: University Press of
Kansas, 2002, pp. 267–304.

Hargrove, Elaine. "Libel News: Silha Center Joins Student
Press Law Center in *Amicus Brief*," Silha Center Bulletin,
10:2 (Minneapolis: University of Minnesota, 2005). http://
www.silha.umn.edu/index.html

"Heed Their Rising Voices" (advertisement), *New York Times*,
March 29, 1960, p. L25.

Henkin, Louis. "Herbert Wechsler," *Proceedings of the American
Philosophical Society*, 146:3 (September 2002), pp. 311–316.

Hudson, David L. Jr. "Online Publishing Forces Evolution of
Defamation Law," First Amendment Center (May 12,
1999). http://www.fac.org/analysis.aspx?id=10479

Jones, Walter B. "Memories of John Brown," *Montgomery
Advertiser*, August 7, 1950.

Kirtley, Jane E. "Criminal Defamation: An 'Instrument of
Destruction,'" Background Paper, School of Journalism and
Mass Communication, University of Minnesota, November
18, 2003.

_____. "It's the Process, Stupid: Newsgathering Is the New
Target," *Columbia Journalism Review* (September/October,
2000). http://archives.cjr.org/year/00/3/kirtley.asp

Kozinski, Alex. "The Bulwark Brennan Built," *Columbia
Journalism Review* 30:4 (November 1, 1991), pp. 1–6.

Krimsky, George A. "The Role of the Media in a Democracy,"
United States Information Agency. http://usinfo.org/
media/press/essay3.htm

Lewis, Anthony. "Court Broadens Freedom of the Press," *New
York Times*, March 15, 1964, p. 10–E.

_____. "High Court Curbs Public Officials in Libel Actions,"
New York Times, March 10, 1964, p. 1.

____. "High Court Extends Protection of First Amendment to Suits Against Papers," *New York Times*, March 11, 1964, p. 20.

____. "The Sullivan Decision," *Tennessee Journal of Law & Policy I*:1 (Fall 2004), pp. 135–151.

____. "Thoughts That We Hate." 1994 Knight Lecture, Stanford University (1994).

Maatman, Mary Ellen. "Working the Devil in the Law of the Land." Widener University School of Law, Paper 786 (2005), pp. 77–78.

McMasters, Paul K. "The crime of speaking ill of your betters," First Amendment Center (November 6, 2005). http://www.firstamendmentcenter.org/commentary.aspx?id=16019

Media Law Resource Center. "Frequently Asked Media Law Questions." New York (2005). http://www.medialaw.org

Miller, Tom. "Tom Paine, the underground press and bloggers," *Los Angeles Times* (August 14, 2005). http://www.latimes.com/news/printedition/suncommentary/la-op-jury14aug14,0,7992374.story?coll=la-headlines-suncomment

Murphy, Doyle. "Organizations join to readdress *Howling Pig* case," *Greeley Tribune* (April 5, 2005). http://www.greeleytrib.com/article/20050405/NEWS/104050057&SearchID=7321634576457

Newhouse Civil Rights and the Press Symposium, "Opening the School House Door: Brown and Its Aftermath," (Syracuse University, April 24, 2004), tape 2. http://civilrightsandthepress.syr.edu/transcripts.html

"Of Reputations and Reporters: A Conference Considers Better Protection for Journalists," *Time* (March 19, 1984). http://www.time.com/time/archive/preview/0,10987,950055,00.html

Paranzino, Gary A. "The Future of Libel Law and Independent Appellate Review: Making Sense of *Bose Corp.* v. *Consumers Union of United States, Inc.*," *Cornell Law Review* (1985). http://paranzino.com/libel.html

Paulson, Ken. "Jailed for speech: Criminal libel is an old—and bad—idea," First Amendment Center (January 18, 2004). http://www.firstamendmentcenter.org/commentary.aspx?id=12468

Pomfret, John D. "Court Broadens Its Rule on Libel," *New York Times*, November 24, 1964, p. 16.

"President Urged to Act in South; Dr. King Asks Intervention to Stop Police 'Terror' in Montgomery Protests," *New York Times*, March 10, 1960, p. 25.

Reed, Ishmael, "The Patriot Act of the 18th Century," *Time* (July 5, 2004). http://www.time.com/time/archive/preview/ 0,10987,1101040705-658357,00.html

Sitton, Claude, "Dr. King Is Seized in Tax Indictment; Atlanta Acts on Alabama's Request—Negro Leader to Fight Extradition," *New York Times*, February 18, 1960, p. 14.

Sloan, David. "John Campbell and the *Boston News-Letter*," *The Early America Review* (2004). http://earlyamerica.com/ review/2005_winter_spring/john_campbell.htm

Solender, Ellen K. "What If" in *Communications Lawyer* (Summer, 1984). Cited in Times *v.* Sullivan *and the Civil Rights Movement* by Lynne Flocke, S. I. Newhouse School of Public Communications, Syracuse University (2003). http://civilrightsandthepress.syr.edu/reflection.html

Student Press Law Center, "Know Your Cybershield: Federal Law Offers online publishers protection from liability denied to their print counterparts," (2000). http://www. splc.org/legalresearch.asp?id=24

"Thomas Jefferson: Establishing a Federal Republic." Library of Congress (Washington, DC: 2001). http://www.loc.gov/ exhibits/jefferson/jefffed.html

"Times Retracts Statement in Ad; Acts on Protest of Alabama Governor over Assertions in Segregation Matter," *New York Times*, May 16, 1960, p. 22.

Wall, Barbara Wartelle. "Legal Watch: Puerto Rico's Criminal Libel Law Declared Unconstitutional." Gannett News Watch. http://www.gannett.com/go/newswatch/2003/ february/nw0214-4.htm

AUDIO

The Center for the Study of Democratic Institutions Audio Archive. Program 123: *Freedom of the Press—I*. Moderated by Robert M. Hutchins; tape numbers A7682/R7, A7683/R7

(May 12, 1964). http://www.library.ucsb.edu/speccoll/csdi/
a7626.html

_____ . Program 124: *Freedom of the Press—II*. Moderated by
Harry Kalven Jr.; tape numbers A7684/R7, A7685/R7 (July
27, 1964). http://www.library.ucsb.edu/speccoll/csdi/
a7684.html

Irons, Peter, ed. *May It Please the Court: Courts, Kids, and the
Constitution*. New York: The New York Press, 2000. Live
recordings and transcripts of the Supreme Court oral arguments.

New York Times v. *Sullivan*, 376 U.S. 254 (1964), docket no. 39.
http://www.oyez.org/oyez/resource/case/277/audioresources

BOOKS/BOOKLETS

*Illinois Press Association Guide to First Amendment and Illinois
Access Laws* (1995). http://www.illinoisfirstamendment
center.com

Ingersoll, Robert G. *The Works of Robert G. Ingersoll*. New York:
Dresden Publishing Company, 1901.

Lewis, Anthony. *Make No Law: The Sullivan Case and the First
Amendment*. New York: Random House, 1991.

McHam, David. *Law & the Media in Texas: Handbook for
Journalists*. Austin: Texas Press Association, 2002.

Paine, Thomas. *Common Sense*. Philadelphia: W. & T Bradford,
1776.

The Reporters Committee for Freedom of the Press. *First
Amendment Handbook*. Arlington, VA, 2003.

Smolla, Rodney A. *Suing the Press: Libel, the Media and Power*.
New York: Oxford University Press, 1986.

Supreme Court Historical Society. "Supreme Court of the United
States" (booklet). http://www.supremecourthistory.org

STATUTES/COURT CASES/DOCUMENTS

Beauharnais v. *Illinois*, 343 U.S. 250 (1952).

Bose Corp. v. *Consumers Union of United States, Inc.*, 466 U.S.
485 (1984).

Bridges v. *California*, 314 U.S. 252 (1941).

Cantwell v. *Connecticut*, 310 U.S. 296 (1940).

Chaplinsky v. *New Hampshire*, 315 U.S. 568 (1942).

Doe v. *Gonzalez* (*Doe* v. *Ashcroft*), 334 F. Supp. 2d 471 (2004).

Garrison v. *Louisiana*, 379 U.S. 64 (1964).

Gertz v. *Robert Welch*, 418 U.S. 323 (1974).

Gitlow v. *People of New York*, 268 U.S. 652 (1925).

Konigsberg v. *State Bar of California*, 366 U.S. 36 (1961).

Near v. *Minnesota*, 283 U.S. 697 (1931).

New York Times v. *Sullivan*, 376 U.S. 254 (1964), including briefs, transcripts, and oral arguments.

1960 Civil Rights Act.

Pennekamp v. *Florida*, 328 U.S. 331 (1946).

Permoli v. *Municipality No. 1 of City of New Orleans*, 44 U.S. 589 (1845).

Rosenbloom v. *Metromedia, Inc.*, 403 U.S. 29 (1971).

Roth v. *United States*, 354 U.S. 476 (1957).

St. Amant v. *Thompson*, 390 U.S. 727 (1968).

Schenck v. *United States*, 249 U.S. 47 (1919).

Sedition Act of 1798.

Senate Commission on Protecting and Reducing Government Secrecy. *Secrecy: A Brief Account of the American Experience* (1997), Senate Document, p. A-57.

Slaughter-House Cases, 83 U.S. 36 (1872).

Terminiello v. *Chicago*, 337 U.S. 1 (1949).

Transcript of proceedings on merits. November 1, 2, and 3, 1960. Circuit Court of Montgomery. *New York Times* v. *Sullivan*, 376 U.S. 254 (1964).

Transcript of records. Alabama Supreme Court. *New York Times* v. *Sullivan*, 376 U.S. 254 (1964).

U.S. Constitution, Articles I, VII, XIV.

Zeran v. *America Online, Inc.*, 129 F.3d 327 (4th Cir. 1997).

WEB SITES

Administrative Office of the U.S. Courts
    http://www.uscourts.gov

American Civil Liberties Union
    http://www.aclu.org

American Civil Liberties Union of Florida
    http://www.aclufl.org

Constitutional Rights Foundation
   http://www.crf-usa.org
Electronic Frontier Foundation
   http://www.eff.org
FindLaw (U.S. Supreme Court Cases)
   http://www.findlaw.com/casecode/supreme.html
First Amendment Center
   http://www.firstamendmentcenter.org
Freedom Forum
   http://www.freedomforum.org
Freedom Forum Special Topic Page: Sullivan at 40 Years
   http://www.firstamendmentcenter.org/faclibrary/case.
   aspx?case=New_York_Times_Co_v_Sullivan
"Heed Their Rising Voices" advertisement
   http://faculty-web.at.northwestern.edu/commstud/
   freespeech/cont/cases/nytsullivan.GIF
Iowa Court Information System
   http://www.judicial.state.ia.us/students/6
JEC Legal Glossary, Judicial Education Center of New Mexico
   http://jec.unm.edu/resources/glossaries/general-
   glossary.htm
Landmark Cases of the U.S. Supreme Court
   http://www.landmarkcases.org
Legal Information Institute, Cornell Law School
   http://www.law.cornell.edu
Library of Congress
   http://memory.loc.gov
Media Law Resource Center
   http://www.medialaw.org
Oyez Project: U.S. Supreme Court Multimedia Web Site
   http://www.oyez.org/oyez/frontpage
Reporters Committee for Freedom of the Press
   http://www.rcfp.org
Supreme Court of the United States
        http://www.supremecourtus.gov
Supreme Court Historical Society
   http://www.supremecourthistory.org

(All Web sites accessible as of November 8, 2005.)

index

Page numbers in **boldface** are illustrations, tables, and charts.

about the author

SUSAN DUDLEY GOLD has written more than three dozen books for middle-school and high-school students on a variety of topics, including American history, health issues, law, and space. Her most recent works for Benchmark Books are *Gun Control* in the Open for Debate series, and *Roe v. Wade: A Woman's Choice?*, *Brown v. Board of Education: Separate but Equal?*, *The Pentagon Papers: National Security or the Right to Know*, *Engel v. Vitale: Prayer in the Schools*, *Korematsu v. United States: Japanese-American Internment*, and *Vernonia School District v. Acton: Drug Testing in the Schools*—all in the Supreme Court Milestones series. She is currently working on two more books about Supreme Court cases.

Susan Gold has also written several books on Maine history. Among her many careers in journalism are stints as a reporter for a daily newspaper, managing editor of two statewide business magazines, and freelance writer for several regional publications. She and her husband, John Gold, own and operate a Web design and publishing business. Susan has received numerous awards for her writing and design work. In 2001 she received a Jefferson Award for community service in recognition of her work with a support group for people with chronic pain, which she founded in 1993. Susan and her husband, also a children's book author, live in Maine. They have one son, Samuel.